Recovery of Reality

SAN DIEGO

Recovery of Reality

Overcoming Chemical Dependency

George A. Mann, M.D.

Published in San Francisco by
HARPER & ROW PUBLISHERS
New York Hagerstown San Francisco London

Designed by Patricia Girvin Dunbar

Library of Congress Cataloging in Publication Data

Mann, George A
    Recovery of reality
    1. Alcoholism — Treatment.   2. Drug abuse — Treatment.
I. Title.
RC565.M258   616.8'6   78-19496
ISBN 0-06-250560-2

86 87 88 89 12 11 10 9 8

This book is dedicated to my wife, Marion Mann, without whose assistance, support, and life it would not have been accomplished. Her presence and her understanding of reality are an ever present source of inspiration and strength.

Contents

Foreword

Within the last decade, the devastation caused by alcoholism and other harmful chemical dependencies has become more and more evident at all levels of our society. As a result, efforts to meet this major health problem have sprung up spontaneously across the country. Virtually every level of national, state and county government has developed some organized program. In the private sector, too, such programs have proliferated. In any major city, one has only to open the telephone book to discover a bewildering array of numbers to call for help.

Yet we live surrounded quite literally by millions who are stricken, who receive no help, and who are moving inexorably toward their premature deaths. They are next door, at work, in our own families. Indeed, they *seek* no help, nor is any sought for them by others.

To this frustrating and deadly truth this book, I believe, addresses itself in a most helpful way. It speaks to those who mistakenly believe that the victims can and will, through spontaneous insight, offer themselves to appropriate care.

Dr. Mann speaks clearly and with concern to those who do not realize that the disease remains hidden within families because the family unit itself is involved in the disease process.

This book is specific and contains easily understood descriptions of viable treatment methods for those who still hold the opinion that "nothing can be done to help them anyway."

Above all, I believe, Dr. Mann offers strong reason for hope to those who have lost all hope and who try as best they can to continue to live in what are becoming increasingly intolerable circumstances.

Dr. Mann appeals particularly to the pragmatist. Not only does he write from a background of medicine, but more particularly from specialized training in anesthesiology. Not only are his observations from personal experience, but from ten years of monitoring the progress of thousands of chemically dependent patients in a highly regarded treatment setting. He writes not so much of what should work, but rather from the proven experience of what *does* work.

I hope many will read this book, for there is help contained in these pages.

Vernon E. Johnson, D.D.
Minneapolis, Minnesota

Acknowledgments

I particularly wish to express my appreciation to Sister Mary Madonna, Chief Executive Officer of St. Mary's Hospital. Her encouragement and support enabled me to adjust a very busy work schedule and devote the time necessary to this effort, and I am truly thankful.

Jim Clayton worked closely with me throughout the development of the manuscript. He provided technical assistance in research, developing material, and editing the copy. We spent hundreds of hours together on this book, and I am grateful for his efforts and assistance.

Phyllis Middlebrook, carefully and with great competence, conducted hours of patient interviews, which served as the basis for the personal case histories in the text. I deeply appreciate her skill and her manner of working with the patients.

I also want to express my thanks to the staff of the Adult Chemical Dependency Unit of St. Mary's Hospital. I was able to devote time to this project because they were willing to support my efforts by understanding and honoring the necessity for my periodic absence. Polly Wadsworth, especially, must be credited with organizing my schedule and working with the staff to make this writing effort possible.

Introduction

I offer this book to the average citizen who has not had the opportunity to observe the day-to-day functioning of a chemical abuse rehabilitation center. What happens inside a treatment center remains a mystery for the largest part of our population. So, first of all, I want to provide a glimpse into the current state of treatment.

Some of you are reading for very personal reasons. You may be concerned about your own behavior or about a close friend or a member of your family. For you there is a very direct and positive message: *Chemical dependency is a treatable disease.* Diagnostic and treatment methods have been tried and tested. People do recover. They regain the ability to live, love, laugh, work, and play. There is hope and help. This message needs to be shouted from the rooftops.

I want to share the experiences of St. Mary's Hospital and Rehabilitation Center, Minneapolis, Minnesota. St. Mary's developed, and has maintained, a very successful program for treatment of chemically dependent people. Its treatment program has a national reputation for excellence, and it needs to be shared with the general population.

As I travel throughout the country, I am constantly amazed that there are still many areas of this nation in which care of the chemically dependent is virtually nonexistent. It is my belief that what has been accomplished by St. Mary's can be undertaken by any hospital, any community, any city, and so by relating St. Mary's experiences I hope to offer encouragement to others who initiate efforts to provide responsible care and treatment.

I also want to write of the prevention of chemical dependency, which is of the utmost importance and must receive greatly increased attention.

It is encouraging to know that chemical dependency can be successfully treated. It is encouraging to know of the concentrated efforts undertaken in many sections of this country resulting in responsible, effective treatment. But responsible treatment has not always been the case.

From the beginning of time, societies have had to deal with chemical dependency. In the nineteenth and twentieth centuries, American society has attempted to deal with chemical dependency through the health-care profession, the church, the legal profession, public education, and social service agencies. Regardless of the social system, the approach has been to place the chemically dependent individual in a position where the only alternatives available were: (1) to attempt to ignore the chemical dependency as much as posisible, or (2) to deal with the individual as though chemical dependency were a manifestation of something else, such as being morally weak, a sinner, a psychotic, a neurotic, or a sociopath.

Prior to 1950, the health-care profession treated the physical and psychiatric complications of dependency rather than dealing directly with the process of dependency itself. The dynamics of chemical dependency were not taught in most medical schools. (This is still true of most medical schools today!) Medical students received lectures on the complications of chemical dependency; they learned about liver disease in its various forms. They learned about the various types of organic brain damage, pancreatitis, nerve damage, gastrointestinal complications, and so on. They heard lectures describing the psychiatric manifestations of chemically dependent behavior. As a result, the average physician graduated from medical school with little understanding about the basic dynamics of chemical dependency.

Consequently, most physicians were quite willing to relegate the case of the chemically dependent person to the psychiatric profession, which basically dealt with chemical dependency as a form of mental illness. Physical internists limited themselves to dealing with the physical complications. Alcoholics were admitted to hospitals on a regular basis, but not for treatment of alcoholism; they were admitted under a wide variety of other diagnoses.

This evasion and indirectness led to grossly inadequate care and a relatively low response to therapy. It came to be a medical axiom that there was nothing to be done for the alcoholic, who was doomed to repeated episodes of uncontrollable drinking, a shortened life expectancy, and a very limited, inadequate level of functioning during that shortened life span.

In 1967, St. Mary's Hospital began to explore alternatives and to ask if a better treatment process, a more effective means of therapy could be developed for the care and ultimate recovery of the chemically dependent.

At that time, there were only a few hospitals offering treatment specifically designed for alcoholism. Existing treatment models were almost all nonmedical. Facilities had been developed and were staffed by individuals who, because of their own insights and intelligence, had experienced recovery from chemical dependency. These people had begun early forms of effective therapy for the treatment of chemical dependency. Most of these people and facilities were associated with Alcoholic Anonymous (AA),[1] which for years successfully worked where the helping professions refused. No single organization has accomplished more for alcoholism recovery than this association of nonprofessional people.

St. Mary's appointed a task force to explore some of the nonmedical treatment methods and to develop a system of treatment that would integrate the existing nonmedical models with available knowledge from the medical world. The Reverend Vernon E. Johnson and members of the Johnson Institute in Minneapolis provided significant input to the task force. Without his efforts, the task force and the alcoholism treatment project would not have completed its work as effectively as it did.

In December 1968, St. Mary's opened its initial treatment facility with sixteen beds. The facility filled rapidly, and pressure for expansion developed immediately. One year later, St. Mary's expanded the program to twenty-five beds. The treatment unit was moved from St. Mary's Hospital to its present location within St. Mary's Rehabilitation Center in 1970. The capacity was again expanded to fifty-three beds in 1973 and, in 1976, to its present capacity of 112 beds.

Although the initial focus of treatment was alcoholism, St. Mary's quickly recognized the need to provide treatment for all forms of chemical dependency. St. Mary's also discovered that the dynamics of chemical dependency and the process of recovery through treatment are the same, regardless of the abused chemical. As discussed later, alcoholism is one form of chemical dependence. Unless specifi-

[1] For readers who are unfamiliar with AA, I recommend *Twelve Steps and Twelve Traditions,* published by Alcoholics Anonymous World Service, Incorporated, New York City. (See also Appendix A for the Twelve Steps on which AA's program is based.)

cally noted the reader can, throughout this book, interchange the term alcoholism with that of chemical dependency and the meaning will not be altered.

As a result of the task force efforts, the program began with a clear understanding that effective treatment must pay close and careful attention to the total person. Treatment of alcoholism could not be conducted by focusing solely on drinking habits and drinking behavior. That approach was too narrow and was doomed to failure. Because alcoholism affects the total life of the individual, treatment had to be developed and implemented that would assist the individual to recover full, healthy functioning in all aspects of living.

The St. Mary's program takes into account the five basic and interrelated dimensions of human beings (see Figure 1). All dimensions are affected in varying degrees by the process of chemical dependency.

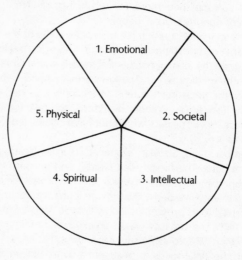

Figure 1

1. There are significant detrimental effects on the *emotional* life of the individual. The process of chemical dependency undermines emotional stability and strength. In *I'll Quit Tomorrow,*[2] the Reverend Vernon Johnson provides a detailed discussion of the Feeling Chart,

---

[2] Vernon E. Johnson, *I'll Quit Tomorrow* (New York: Harper & Row, 1973).

which graphically represents the range of human emotions and feelings.

Pain	*Feeling Chart* Normal	Euphoria
-10 -9 -8 -7 -6 -5	-4 -3 -2 -1 0 1 2 3 4	5 6 7 8 9 10

Most people will live most of their lives within the mid-range of this graph. Individuals may be a bit "down" or a bit "up," but most of the time they are neither extremely happy nor extremely sad. As emotional pain increases, people will manage their lives in a way to decrease the pain and move back into the mid-range. Most people experience degrees of euphoria, but these experiences tend to be short-lived, and the individual returns to the mid-range.

The process of chemical dependency results in the individual's moving further and further to the left on the Feeling Chart. Emotional dysphoria — being emotionally down — becomes the common state. Whether or not the individual is under the influence of alcohol or other mood-altering chemicals at any given time, he or she will continue to experience painful emotional feelings rather than returning to the mid-range. Guilt, shame, anxiety, depression, anger, hostility, and resentment become the individual's constant emotional state.

The recovery process must enable the individual to reestablish, to regain, the ability to live with healthy emotions and feelings. The recovery process must work to develop a sense of personal self-worth, respect, integrity, strength, and stability.

2. The *societal* aspects of the individual will deteriorate. The individual's ability to develop and sustain interpersonal relationships is significantly undermined. Relationships with other people disintegrate as chemical dependency increases. The number of friends will decrease; old friendships will be terminated. Family life will be jeopardized and eventually destroyed. A sense of loneliness and isolation will increase. The chemically dependent person must learn to reinstitute, or to develop for the first time, relationships that are healthy and supportive. Only through relationships with other people will loneliness and isolation be decreased.

3. The process of chemical dependency reduces and limits *intellectual* ability. For example, reading comprehension, mathematical skills, and reasoning ability are diminished. Test scores will continue to decrease, and grades will begin to drop for the student. The A

student will have to work hard for Bs and Cs. The employee will have to spend more energy performing tasks that used to be easy.

Other changes also take place. The process of chemical dependency results in basic changes in the ability to remember and to recall. The sense of time becomes confused; one hour blends into the next, one day blends into the next. Recall of events becomes vague.

With proper treatment, it is possible for the individual to regain most of the intellectual ability he or she had attained before the onset of chemical dependency. The sense of time can be reestablished; memory and recall will begin to return. The degree of recovery is directly related to the extent of brain damage suffered as a result of chemical dependency.

4. There are significant detrimental effects to the *spiritual* life of the chemically dependent person. The individual will experience a sense of isolation from God. As this sense of isolation grows, the individual will become more confused, with a further deterioration of the ability to cope with chemical dependency. Eventually the chemically dependent person will lose the ability to have any true concept of God. The experience of social isolation has its counterpart in the existential experience of being isolated from any understanding of a benevolent or loving God.

The individual will also engage in activities which conflict with his or her value system. Destructive behaviors will increase, the individual will begin doing and saying things that would have been unacceptable prior to the onset of chemical dependency. If unchecked, the process of chemical dependency will result in the individual's inability to choose between right or wrong, good or bad. The individual will experience a profound sense of remorse and guilt but will continue to violate his or her sense of what is acceptable behavior.

5. The individual is affected *physically.* There are many medical complications resulting from the process of chemical dependency. Many diseases tend to coexist with chemical dependency, and there is an increased incidence of diabetes, hypertension, heart disease, liver and pancreatic disease, and cancer. All of these physical manifestations must be treated in order for the individual to achieve a full and meaningful life.

A complete range of medical services must be available for the patient. St. Mary's medical staff works closely with the admitting physician to assure competent health care for physical diseases and psychiatric illnesses. Specialists are available for consultation with the patient and the admitting physician, thereby providing the full dimensions of health care.

The whole person must be treated. If we concentrate simply on drinking or other drug experiences, then the whole person does not get well. We must concern ourselves with the five dimensions of the human being and the way they are affected by chemical dependency.

From the inception of St. Mary's In-Patient Program, there has also been a two-year Aftercare Program, which supports and continues the treatment begun in the In-Patient Program. Aftercare works with the patient's spouse and children, in the case of married couples or with individuals who are significant to the single patient's recovery.

In 1973, we began an Out-Patient Program that provides treatment for the individual who is less disabled, who is able to maintain a fairly responsible level of functioning in the world, but still is in need of therapy. The average length of time spent in the Out-Patient Program is one month.

We also discovered that there are individuals who are profoundly affected by the dependency process and are extremely dysfunctional. These people need far more care than the average individual. Many of these people have no family or no significant people in their lives who can provide stability. To meet the needs of these individuals and to provide responsible treatment, Talbot Hall, a halfway house, was established. Talbot Hall is named after Matt Talbot, revered as the Irish "saint" of alcoholism.

We must recognize that chemical dependency is a treatable disease. It is a progressive disease, that is, the longer the disease process remains untreated, the more severe will be the consequences. If left untreated, chemical dependency will frequently result in premature death. With treatment, however, there is a high rate of recovery.

Chemical dependency not only leads to the destruction of the individual, it also is a significant force in generating illness in the family and friends of the chemically dependent person. The families, the associates, the partners and friends of the chemically dependent person suffer the side effects of the illness. Therefore, treatment is appropriate not only for chemically dependent individuals but also for the other people most directly affected by the illness. In response to this need, a family therapy program was initiated at St. Mary's in the spring of 1977.

Frequently the chemically dependent person is labelled immoral and irresponsible and is accused of rationally choosing chemical use and abuse over family, friends, and work. Much of this attitude arises from the fact that people close to the chemically dependent person do suffer, their lives are destructively affected. Also, it appears as though the dependent person does consciously choose to wreck his or her life. But appearances are deceiving. The chemically dependent person has lost the ability to leave chemicals alone, and is out of control. Treatment must be organized in such a way as to enable the individual patient to increase the element of control. This is not accomplished by calling the patient immoral and irresponsible.

There are still many places in our society where the typical approach to the disease of chemical dependency is to admit the individual into a hospital for detoxification; institute nutrition and vitamin therapy; prescribe mood-controlling medications; and then put the patient back on the street, back home, or back on the job, and back to destructive drinking. There is a defeatist attitude in this behavior that says nothing significant can be done for the chemically dependent person. If this attitude prevails, the person and the people who love that person will come to believe that they have no way to influence the course of the destructive process. The chemically dependent population experiences high divorce rates, destructive behavior, repeated hospitalizations, and a high rate of suicide.

Too often, the advice the alcoholic receives from the physician is that he or she drinks too much and should cut back or quit drinking and go on some medication. This approach is doomed to failure. The physician becomes discouraged and disenchanted because the results are very poor. The alcoholic and the alcoholic's family become discouraged because they do not perceive success. Both the patient and the physician find themselves in a no-win method of treatment.

However, when chemically dependent individuals receive well-planned therapy, approximately 60-75 percent will recover. These individuals will return to full function, full life expectancy, and the opportunity for growth and development that previously was not possible.

A vast amount of knowledge has been acquired through studies, research, and experience at St. Mary's. Relying on St. Mary's knowledge, this book is organized to answer four basic questions frequently asked by friends and family of the chemically dependent person:

1. *Why does chemical dependency occur, and what happens within the process of chemical dependency?* First, we will examine answers to these questions by looking at the influences of our own society and by examining how other cultures and other societies have attempted to deal with chemical dependency. Next, we will examine chemical dependency as a disease process affecting the totality of the

individual and all involved people. Relevant background materials from psychology and physiology are presented to answer the questions of "why" and "what happens."

2. *How can the process of chemical dependency be diagnosed?* One misconception is that everyone who misuses or abuses alcohol is an alcoholic. Chemical dependency is a specific, identifiable disease entity. There are ways to determine whether or not mood-altering drugs are disrupting the individual's ability to adequately function. So we will deal not only with the diagnosis of chemical dependency but also with other identifiable processes involving chemical abuse that need to be understood.

3. *What happens in treatment?* Treatment is too important to be surrounded by mystery and mythology. The specific methodology, dynamics, and procedures employed by St. Mary's Adult Chemical Dependency Treatment Program will be thoroughly described, providing a clear picture of what happens in treatment and removing a lot of the mystery surrounding treatment.

4. *What can we do to prevent chemical dependency?* Chemical dependency is a preventable process. We will examine some of the factors causing chemical dependency and present a programmatic approach that can result in the prevention of chemical dependency.

This book addresses the subject of chemical dependency with the hope that those people who are now chemically dependent will receive adequate treatment to prevent the destruction of their own lives and the lives of those around them, and that prevention efforts will be greatly increased so that those who are presently abusing chemicals or who are potential abusers will find ways to live more productively and short-circuit the trip into chemical dependency.

Finally, patients have been interviewed and their stories are included in case histories. The reader should understand that all material has been screened to assure the privacy of these very special people. They are special not because of their occupations, but because they are willing to share their own experiences with the hope that they will prove helpful to you.

George A. Mann, M.D.
Minneapolis, Minnesota

I Overview

1 Culture and Chemicals

Thousands of people – patients, family members, friends – have participated in the St. Mary's treatment program. They have come from every region of the United States and represent a wide range of occupations and work skills. Some are professionals such as physicians, clergy, attorneys, and school teachers. Others are highly trained engineers, business executives, and government leaders. Still others are housewives, auto mechanics, students, sales clerks. Our patients are the kind of people who live in most neighborhoods of this nation.

Chemical dependency is not restricted to any particular age group, any particular sex, any particular occupation, any income level. Nor is any grouping of people in this country automatically immune to chemical dependency.

In other cultures, there have been groups of people where a clearly identifiable process of chemical abuse did not exist. This is true of the original Eskimo culture; for centuries the Eskimo people lived without the destructive consequences of chemical abuse. Similarly, for hundreds of years the North American Indians maintained a civilization free of chemical abuse. Anthropologists have discovered other isolated cultures that existed for centuries without the societal problems associated with chemical abuse.

In every one of these cases, however, whenever alcohol was introduced to the culture, within a generation or two alcoholism has rapidly become a major social problem.

It is easy to trace historical patterns of chemical abuse within civilizations and cultures. Each culture has attempted to control the

3

use of chemicals and has attempted to solve societal problems related to chemical abuse through its laws, taboos, regulations, and religious codes. Archaeologists have reconstructed codes of law regulating personal and societal behavior related to chemicals, including regulations for the sale of alcoholic beverages. For example, in Babylonian culture, under the guidance and leadership of Hammurabi in the sixteenth and seventeenth centuries B.C., one of the most famous codes of law was developed. The Code of Hammurabi illustrates early attempts to regulate and control the purchase and use of alcoholic beverages.[1]

The ways in which cultures have dealt with the social problems related to alcohol abuse is clearly traceable through the Sumerian and Babylonian cultures and on through the many Egyptian dynasties, the various phases of the Greek and Roman Empires, more recently in the British Empire, and today in our own society. Each of these cultures has struggled to control chemical abuse and to formulate social policies penalizing abuse while permitting responsible use. In this respect, our society is no different. Throughout our brief history as a nation, we have attempted to deal with the problems of chemical abuse in two basic ways.

First, we have a legal history in which we have attempted to find the right combination of laws to penalize antisocial behavior related to chemical abuse and to define responsible adult use. In the case of alcohol, we have our history of prohibition and our current situation of legally defined manufacture, sale, and consumption. The number of federal and state regulations continues to increase. Public pressure is mounting for even more restrictive and more clearly defined legal controls and legal penalties.

However, we are a very inconsistent nation when we look at the laws and regulations regarding the use of mood-altering drugs. For example, there is mounting pressure for more controls on the use of alcohol and, at the same time, a strong lobby to reduce the controls on the use of marijuana. Although the federal government has not eased the rules and restrictions for marijuana, many state legislatures are decriminalizing its possession and use. We do not have a clearcut social policy in this country. Efforts directed to the reduction of chemical dependency must be conducted with the clear knowledge

---

[1] Robert Francis Harper, *The Code of Hammurabi, King of Babylon* (Chicago: University of Chicago Press, 1904), p. 37, paragraphs 108–110.

that laws and social policy are in a state of flux and will shift and change.

In the second place, our society has attempted to control chemical abuse through moral and religious persuasion. Within the world of organized religion, restrictions range all the way from complete abstinence to the responsible consumption of alcohol. In some faith groups, you are immoral and a sinner if you consume any alcoholic beverages. In other faith groups, you are immoral and a sinner only if you become an abusive drinker or an alcoholic.

Although religious organizations carry on the debate with each other as to whether or not a believer can consume alcoholic beverages, they have a far more basic value system in common; namely, they believe the alcoholic is guilty of sin and immorality. The alcoholic has chosen the bottle over belief. This may sound harsh, but it accurately reflects the experience of most people who have participated in the St. Mary's program.

While efforts continue to achieve better and more effective laws related to chemical dependency, and while religious organizations continue to convert people to one faith or another, neither law nor religion seems to have much effect in reducing the numbers of people who experience alcoholism and other forms of chemical dependency. The answer to the question, "Why does someone use a mood-altering substance to the point of chemical dependency?" will not be found in a discussion of our current laws, nor will it be found in efforts of moral persuasion.

The "why" of chemical dependency is to be understood in the careful examination of two separate but related sources of information. We must pay attention to what is known about human development, and we must understand what is there about mood-altering substances that will affect an individual's sense of reality.

Why will someone abuse a mood-altering substance to the point of chemical dependency? The answer to this question lies in the interrelationship existing between the individual and the chemical. How does that individual view himself or herself? How does the individual perceive and respond to reality? What are the predictable physiological effects of mood-altering substances? These are the important factors in the development of chemical dependency.

Mood-altering substances are chemicals, and, as such, they have predictable effects on the mind and the body. Chemical dependency is the result of chemical reactions within the central nervous system

(CNS). For example, alcoholism is the result of how alcohol affects the CNS and the subsequent personality changes of the individual. Once the process of chemical dependency has begun, the individual experiences less and less control over mood and behavior and develops behavior patterns peculiar to this process. The process of chemical dependency will eventually determine and control the individual's behavior; the affected individual experiences fewer and fewer conscious behavior controls.

How does this come about? Why is it that some people can consume alcoholic beverages without suffering the damaging effects of alcoholism but the process of chemical dependency is established in other people? To answer these questions about chemical dependency, let's first look at how personality is developed.

2 Personality and Mood-Altering Chemicals

Carol: *Married, with children, in her mid-forties:*

I had my first drink at 17. When I was a young girl it was unheard of to drink in high school. So I had my first beer after I went to college. I remember having to learn to like it; at first I didn't like the taste of it.

I got into trouble right off the bat, as soon as I started going to beer parties. I crawled out of the dorm window my freshman year and got caught. . . . I was placed on disciplinary probation.

I always made good grades in college. But college was not only good grades. I went to lots of parties and had lots of fun. At that time the drinking was an awful lot of fun. I remember very well the first time I got drunk. I went out with a friend, and we decided to live it up and have a good time. I got horribly drunk. He took me home and I was so drunk I couldn't get up to my bedroom. I passed out on the living room couch. My mother found me, and I recall her telling me not to say anything to my dad. We kept it a secret from him.

My husband and I were married just after we graduated from college. I always had a drink before dinner, and I recall he didn't like that. At that time all we could afford to buy was beer and an occasional bottle of gin. On weekends and special occasions I'd fix a gin and tonic, but normally all I drank was beer.

My husband went into the armed forces, so we started moving around a lot. Of course we always went to the base club. They always held a happy hour on Friday when drinks were 25¢ each. That's where I really got started on martinis.

When my husband was discharged we moved back to my home town, and my husband went to work with my father. My drinking pattern stayed about the same. We went to lots of parties and did lots of drinking. This went on for about six years. During this time I was regularly getting drunk at every party.

We were having marital problems, so we went into counseling. We decided for our future that we needed to be away from the influence of my parents. So we moved to another state, and my husband started his own business. My drinking pattern continued: lots of parties and lots of drinking.

We moved again to another city when my husband got a job in sales management. He did very well, and the parties became more frequent. My drinking became heavier. I was having two or three drinks at home each day and always getting drunk at the parties. I was also regularly taking sleeping pills and I was drinking heavily by myself.

I remember I went to a friend's house to play bridge. After I arrived I started to shake all over. My whole body was shaking and jerking. I told the women it was because I was on a diet and wasn't eating well. They put me in a bedroom so I could rest while the game continued. They called me when lunch was served. We had wine for lunch, and the shaking stopped. This happened twice within three months. The only way I could calm myself was with a glass of wine or some other drink.

Then it really became worse, I stopped all daytime activities because I was afraid to go anyplace. I would shake violently unless I had a drink. This shaking happened to me several times in the supermarket. I'd be calm when I left home, but when I'd try to write a check to pay for the groceries I would be overcome with shaking. I know people had to notice, my whole body would be shaking. I began to write my checks at home when I needed to go to the store. Then I would just hand the written check to the cashier. That way people wouldn't see how much trouble it was for me to write.

By this time my whole day revolved around drinking. I couldn't go anyplace or do anything without being fortified with my drinks. I'd have a few drinks in the morning, write my checks, do my shopping, then come home and have another drink. By now I was drinking close to a quart per day.

I was still getting drunk at parties, but now I was experiencing blackouts; I couldn't remember what I'd done at the party.

I tried to control my drinking. All day I would alternate drinking iced tea and then an alcohol drink. I didn't want to be drunk when my husband came home. But I always was, because by mid-afternoon I had forgotten about the iced tea.

I stopped associating with people who didn't drink. Old friends were long gone. I only wanted to be with people who drank. The only reason I wanted to go out during the day time was to play bridge so I could drink wine.

My family had been after me for some time to get into treatment. I was making life miserable for everyone. One weekend my husband was out of town and I found myself up at 5:30 A.M. pouring a drink. I had a horrible day because if frightened me that I would get up at 5:30 in the morning to drink. I was terrified. I knew the name of St. Mary's treatment center, so I called them. They scheduled me to enter on the next Wednesday. I cried all day long. From that Saturday until the following Wednesday I drank all I could. I couldn't get enough.

But I had my last drink on the day I entered treatment.

Recently I was talking with our oldest son about one of my drunken visits to his college on Mother's Day. He really shocked me because he said he had been stoned on marijuana the whole weekend. What I had to tell him was that I was stoned on alcohol the whole weekend. We were both so drunk on our own drugs that we didn't know the other one was acting strangely.

There are many ways to understand and to talk about the development of human personality. There are many approaches to discussing how and why people grow up to be the way they are. One approach that makes sense is looking at human development from the standpoint of individuals learning to cope with reality, learning ways to deal with what is happening in their lives, learning to live with the world around them. The development of coping skills, the growing ability to deal with more and more complex situations, is one of the most important goals of human development.

Prenatal

While in the womb, the soon-to-be-born infant lives in an entirely protective world, a world of immediate and constant gratification. Nourishment is ever present, waste elimination is automatic, the environment is warm and sheltered. This is the only time that human beings will live in a completely protective environment, live without the awareness of pain and frustration, and live with every need satisfied.

Infancy

At birth all is changed. For the first time, needs are not automatically and consistently met. Nourishment, which previously had been supplied through the mother's bloodstream, must be sought. The infant experiences hunger and must behave in such a way as to satisfy the need. Elimination of waste products, a function previously performed by the mother's body, is now an act experienced by the infant. The environment is no longer automatically maintained. The infant experiences the displeasure of heat, cold, hunger, skin irritations, and so on. All of these changes occur dramatically and instantaneously at the time of birth.

The newborn infant is immediately thrust into a reality demanding growth and maturity. The infant must develop coping skills to a level sufficient to meet his or her needs. As we shall see later, an inadequate capacity for coping is one of the major factors influencing the process of chemical dependency.

Fortunately for both the child and the parents, the process of physical maturity is already underway. The infant quickly learns to distinguish the needs for food, waste elimination, warmth, or coolness. The infant is capable of voicing pleasure and displeasure. However, throughout this period, the infant is still totally dependent upon other people for satisfaction of needs.

Childhood

From infancy through childhood, the task is to identify basic needs and learn ways for those needs to be satisfied. During this time, the personality of the child is in its most formative stages. The groundwork for identity is laid. Images of self-identity are developed. What other people think about the child, how other people behave with the child, and the experiences of pain and pleasure are imprinted into the child's personality. The child attempts to learn how to cope with the world and experiences living with other people. This means that every wish, every demand, every need will be met, be partially met, or remain unmet in relationship with other people. The child quickly learns to manipulate the outside world for the gratification of needs and wants.

One of the major responsibilities of parents is aiding the child in learning how to live with other human beings, how to receive satisfaction for wants and desires from other people. This learning is not just rational and intellectual. Emotional learning also occurs and establishes patterns for future behavior.

It is extremely important for the child to learn ways to satisfy basic needs and wants. It is also crucial for the child to learn to cope with those situations where basic needs and wants will be only partially fulfilled or not fulfilled at all. The kinds of lessons the child learns in these situations, how well the child can cope with frustration, has a lot to do with the continued health and growth of the child. The child is learning what to do when needs are unmet, when life is not going as he or she desires. The emotional learning taking place during this period of life is crucial for the subject of chemical dependency.

It is my clinical judgment that chemically dependent individuals have not developed adequate coping skills to help them endure high levels of pain and frustration resulting from unmet needs. The emotional learning of early childhood is deeply imprinted into the personality of every one of us. For some, this emotional learning provides strength and support for coping with crisis, anger, frustration, and so on. For others, the emotional learning is not nearly so productive and has not resulted in strength or increased coping skills. Chemical dependency may develop when an individual begins to use mood-altering substances as an alternative way of coping with the harshness of reality.

The need for satisfaction and gratification is also intertwined with the need for love and approval, a strong driving force in the emotional life of a child. The child learns ways to cope with the tension that exists when he or she wants something and the parents expect different behavior. How the child learns to cope with tension and behaves to reduce it is an important factor in the learning of coping skills. The parent is constantly teaching, directing, guiding, and expecting. The parent attempts to meet the needs of the child and, at the same time, attempts to convey that all needs cannot be met immediately, that living means learning to live with tension and conflict.

The child must also learn that some needs will never be met. Very quickly the child learns that life includes the presence of anxiety. How the child learns to cope with anxiety, to manipulate the world to reduce anxiety, is learning carried forward throughout life.

One of the most prevalent personality characteristics of individuals suffering from chemical dependency is an ongoing inability to cope with pervasive anxiety. For some such people, the anxiety level is extreme and intolerable. For others, the anxiety level is not centered on any particular set of activities but is generalized and always present. In the case of the alcoholic, alcohol is frequently used initially to relieve anxiety.

The ability to find relief and to cope with anxiety has a direct relationship to the development of chemical dependency. The individual who has developed skills to cope with anxiety is less likely to become chemically dependent. The individual who uses mood-altering substances to cope with anxiety is running a greater risk of developing chemical dependency. Childhood learning of how to cope with anxiety has a direct bearing on the development of chemical dependency.

One of the most common ways to escape the reality of anxiety is in daydreaming and fantasy. This is a coping mechanism the child learn very early. It is easier to daydream of being all-powerful than it is to deal with the reality of limited power. It is easier to daydream of totally and forever loving parents than it is to live with the reality that parents are human beings subject to failure. It is easier to daydream of having a pony and every other possible gift than it is to live with the reality that what you have is all there is. One task of the parent is to present reality to the child and to aid in the learning of coping skills that will enable the child to live with reality, a reality that includes pain as well as pleasure and loss as well as gain.

The matter of fantasy life must be kept in perspective. Fantasizing is not necessarily harmful, nor is it necessarily destructive to the individual's ability to cope and function. For many people, fantasy is productive and health producing. Fantasizing becomes a danger primarily when the distinction between fantasy and reality is lost, when the individual comes to believe that his or her fantasy life is in fact a representation of the here and now.

The child grows and matures, dealing with hope and despair. The child experiences the developing belief that most sought after desires and wishes can fulfilled. The child will also experience unfulfilled needs and wishes, reacting in anger with tears, fighting and retreat. The child must experience denial as well as fulfillment in order to begin the process of differentiating between desires that can be fulfilled and those that probably will not be. As an extremely self-centered human being, the child is attempting to mature and grow in the development of a will: a will to do, a will to have, and a will to be.

These struggles result in the learning of self-identity. The degree to which the learning is positive is the degree to which the individual begins to develop a good self-image. If the learning is negative, if despair overrides hope, if frustration overrides pleasure, then these become the dominant themes in self-identity.

The child also develops the restraints and the controls to live as a member of the family and the skill and courage to identify and to pursue desires even in the face of punishment and rejection. The child is developing physical dexterity and other abilities while at the same time experiencing failure and frustration. For the child, reality is a series of opposites: love and rejection, success and failure, reality and fantasy, enthusiasm and indifference, feelings of power and weakness. Many adults indicate that this list is not much different from adult experience. In many respects, they are correct. However, we need to remember that the child begins with no experience in coping with the tension existing between these opposites. There is a first time for experiencing these opposites, and that time is childhood. The first learning becomes the foundation for all that follows.

Adolescence

The emotional learning acquired during childhood is carried into adolescence and adulthood. Further growth and development are constructed on earlier learning. The ability or inability to deal with pressure, to cope with high levels of anxiety or frustration are directly related to the potential development of chemical dependency. If mood-altering chemicals are used because of a breakdown or absence of coping abilities, the physiological effects of the chemical will eventually take over and lead directly to chemical dependency. How the child responds and learns to cope with frustration and anxiety has a direct bearing on future experimentation and learning with mood-altering chemicals.

These same dynamics continue through adolescence. They become stronger and more pronounced because the adolescent is adding a level of sophistication and discernment as a result of previous life experiences. The opposites become more pronounced. Another dynamic, another level of experience, is incorporated into the developmental growth of the adolescent. It is during this time of

life that development of interpersonal relationships outside the immediate family becomes exceedingly important. It is as though the urge is
to give total allegiance to friends. It is during this stage of development that the individual needs to develop and sustain deep friendships, which obviously result in a great deal of pleasure and comfort.
The development of friendship and loyalty provides the base for
growth and maturation.

Just as in childhood, the very urge to create and sustain loyalties
and friendships results in the experiences of broken loyalties and lost
friendships. At the very time when the "I" is emotionally nurtured by
the creation of deep friendships, the "I" is most vulnerable to
rejection and feelings of loneliness. If the struggle for friendship is
painful and is only partially successful or results in failure, the emotional stability is undercut and the "I" suffers. The adolescent is learning
that deep and loyal friendships are extremely important to his or her
well-being. The adolescent also experiences the element of risk in
attempts to develop these sustaining relationships. The adolescent
suffers the risk of rejection, the risk of failure, the risk of loneliness.
The adolescent has the opportunity to learn by experience, to acquire
and to incorporate skills that make it possible to cope with anguish
and loneliness.

It is crucial to remember that experimentation with mood-altering
chemicals usually begins during adolescence. It is generally during this
period that consumption of alcoholic beverages is begun. Whether
on a bet, on a dare, of for the fun of it, most adolescents will
experiment with alcohol or other mood-altering chemicals. It is now,
for example, that experimentation with marijuana usually occurs.
From the standpoint of personality development, the danger of
experimenting with alcohol or marijuana during this time arises from
the fact that these chemicals are, in fact, very effective toward
inducing a mood and a frame of mind that is very peaceful and
satisfying to the adolescent. The adolescent is undergoing an internal
civil war. The emotional struggle of Dr. Jekyll and Mr. Hyde is normal
and should be expected. It is most essential, however, for the
adolescent to experience development and growth in terms of self-
identity and the ability to cope with tension and frustration. The use
of alcohol or marijuana will reduce the amount of anxiety experienced by the adolescent and will make the world seem light and
happy, even though reality is very painful. Mood-altering chemicals
are just as effective in reducing emotional pain and stress for the

adolescent as they are for the adult. One of the major dangers of mood-altering chemicals is that, by the use of these substances, the adolescent may miss the opportunity to discover new coping skills or to further develop existing skills and strengths. .

This view of human development should not be seen as negative or pessimistic. It is one way of looking at what everyone experiences. Everyone learns how to cope with reality, to deal with what is going on in life. Most people develop coping skills that are adequate to make the experience of life pleasurable, or at least tolerable. When the experience of reality is tough or painful, some people have coping skills that enable them to deal with the pain and the frustration of these situations. For instance, what happens when:

- your car runs out of gas at a busy intersection?
- you have a flat tire on the highway?
- a young child spills the third plateful of food on the floor at the same meal?
- you get behind in your work, and the pressure is mounting for that work to be completed?
- your teen-age son or daughter is consistently late returning home from a date?
- your child receives failing grades in school?
- you have tremendous financial pressure from unpaid bills?
- your spouse, child, or closest friend becomes severely ill?

Most of the time, most people deal with these situations, handle the frustration, and go about the daily task of living. What happens, though, when events occur that produce a great deal of stress, such as a death in the family; divorce; children growing up and leaving home; or the loss of a job? These events are stress-producing, and for some people chemicals play a significant part in reducing the stress. Each of us has developed our own ways of coping with stress.

There is another important aspect of learning to cope with reality. Most of us learned to cope by observing our parents. If you stop to examine your behavior, you will probably find that your actions often duplicate your own parents' behavior. How you deal with decision making, how you deal with happiness, how you deal with frustration look a lot like your folks when they were your age.

Each of us has learned our lessons well. We have learned from those people who have been most significant in our lives, no matter whether our experience of those people is negative or positive. There is a great deal of similarity between our behavior and theirs.

We are not exact carbon copies, but we are alike in a great many ways – and one of those ways is how we cope with frustration and pain.

Infants and young children learn most from the adult or adults with whom they live. For most of us, this means our parents. For others, it means an aunt, an uncle, or a foster parent. Whatever the case may be, those significant adults not only provided us food and shelter, they gave us models of how to live. We begin to develop our value system of what is good or bad, a sense of right or wrong, the basis for determining what is important and unimportant by trying to be like those significant adults. That is the only way we know how to behave. We model ourselves and our behavior after those people.

How many times have you been embarrassed or seen other parents embarrassed because of the language a young child uses in front of grandparents? And how many times have you given or heard the excuse that the child must have learned the language from the neighborhood kids? Granted, children do pick up language patterns from other playmates. But at age two or three, they are saying what their parents say. And it doesn't take them long to know what to say when they make a mistake or when they are angry.

Just as they learn their language from us, children also learn from us how to deal with conflict and anxiety-producing situations. They observe the people around them, and they learn from that observation. Initially they cry if they are hungry. If they need their diaper changed, they cry. If they are tired, they cry.

This coping with reality continues for a while as a natural response of the infant. But it doesn't take long for major learning to occur. The infant-child learns quickly there are other ways to have needs met. Children will experiment with a wide range of behaviors, learning how people around them respond to the behavior. They cry, and, if that doesn't work, hold their breath until they are red in the face. Then comes the tantrum. They will hit. They will argue. They will run out of the room and hide. They will try being passive, that "I don't care" attitude. This learning process is the normal evolution of adequate coping mechanisms.

Children also learn their parents' attitudes toward the use of mood-altering chemicals. Just as the child will model parental language, the child will also model parental behavior and attitude when it comes to dealing with pain and frustration. If children see a parent using medication of one form or another to get through the day, they will learn quickly to use medicine or mood-altering chemicals as a help for problems. Children learn these lessons from routine, everyday experiences.

Parents do not have to be chemically dependent in order for children to learn attitudes that can be destructive later in life. It may be as simple an act as always using aspirin for the slightest headache or always responding to the child's physical and emotional pain with some form of medication. If the parent is able to cope with emotional pain in nonchemical ways, again, the child will learn by example. Children copy the behavior of their parents.

As a result of all their experiences, children learn to cope adequately or inadequately with reality. For example, they learn how to live with the other people around them harmoniously or in conflict. In the beginning, this learning is not rational or intellectual. The child doesn't have words to put with feelings; it is an emotional learning. It is a base of learning upon which the child relies for future growth and development. The child learns what works and what doesn't work. Later on, the child learns to differentiate between situations. What works one place won't work in another, so the child's range of behavior is broadened and expanded.

This emotional learning will be carried through adolescence and into adulthood. Our ability to cope with reality will continue to be tested, and the healthy person will have a reservoir of coping skills sufficient to meet trying situations. The lessons learned through the experience of coping with reality keep most people healthy most of the time.

Each of us has different levels of coping ability. An event that would seem quite ordinary and non-stress-producing to one individual may well be the breaking point for someone else. We each have our own reservoir of limited strength. The ability to tolerate unpleasant reality and to work for the reduction and resolution of the tension it produces are not automatically present at birth; they are skills that must be learned.

From the moment of birth, through infancy, childhood, adolescence, and into adulthood, coping skills must be developed and refined. There is no point when the individual has developed all the coping skills and mechanisms needed to sustain life. Unfortunately, the use of mood-altering chemicals can arrest human growth and the development of these crucial skills.

3 Motivation and Chemical Dependency

Abraham Maslow, a psychologist noted for his research and work in understanding human development, offers another way of describing human personality.[1] He has developed a framework for understanding the motivation of people. One way of answering the question, "Why do people behave as they do?" is to look at human experience in terms of what an individual needs in order to be a healthy, mature human being. Maslow proposes that there is a hierarchy of basic human needs. This is a good way of understanding the human personality as a very complex organism, in which all the parts are interrelated. He suggests that there are five groupings or clusters of human needs, represented by the pyramid shown in Figure 2. Maslow's way organizing human personality makes sense in our experience at St. Mary's. There are exceptions of course, but this grouping of human needs represents a good way of presenting general statements about most people. Our experience indicates that, as one grouping of needs is largely met, the individual then has the energy and time to live and work at the next level. If basic *physiological* needs are met, if the individual has enough food, clothing, and shelter to sustain his or her life, then the bare minimum has been met and the primary need becomes that of security.

Security involves both physical and emotional needs. It may be the

[1] Abraham H. Maslow, *Motivation and Personality* (New York: Harper & Row 1954).

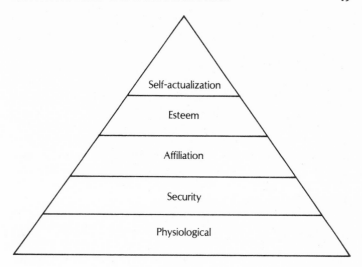

Figure 2

drive to be secure in your job, to know that you have a reasonable chance to enter retirement with enough money for food, clothing, and shelter. It may mean that you are reasonably sure that the chance of catastrophic illness is remote; therefore, you don't worry about it. It may mean that you view life in such a way so you don't worry about what you can't control; you don't worry about tomorrow.

The next level is that of *affiliation*, or belonging, of loving and being loved, of knowing you belong with other people

After this comes the grouping of needs of *esteem*, including esteem received from others as well as self-esteem. At this level, individuals know who they are, accept themselves for who they are, and have a clear idea of their abilities and limitations.

The development of a strong sense of self-identity, the presence of a strong ego enables the individual to move into the fifth level, that of *self-actualization*. This means accomplishing one's full potential. Self-actualizing people live with a sense of realizing their full potential as human beings. There is a danger here of confusing this with being successful. To live with one's full potential actualized will mean something different for every individual. It doesn't mean that you are the best in a particular occupation or task. It does mean that you are operating in an area where you have the potential to live to your fullest capacity emotionally, socially, intellectually, spiritually, and physically.

The drive to fulfill these needs is a very definite force within each person.

First, keep in mind that all five areas are interrelated. No one person operates at just one level. Many activities will contribute to the meeting of needs in all five areas. For example, employment will provide the money to secure the basic physiological needs of food, clothing, shelter. Money earned from employment is also used to meet the needs for security. Employment for some people provides the arena for interpersonal relationships and friendships. Self-esteem and a strong sense of self-identity may be enhanced through employment. And certainly for some people, employment is one of the arenas for giving expression to one's full capacities and in which one develops self-actualization. In these terms, employment should be understood in the broadest possible context. The dynamics can be the same whether we're thinking about a college student, a factory worker, a professional, or a mother or father whose primary role is in the home.

Secondly, although all are interrelated, most people will experience one of the groupings as dominant and the other four as secondary. The grouping of needs that dominate today may not be the same next week. Life changes require a shifting of focus, a shifting of what is important to the individual. This is readily apparent when you talk with someone whose employment has just been terminated, one in the hospital recovering from a serious accident or illness, one whose spouse or child or significant friend is in the hospital, or the individual who is directly involved in the termination of a marriage.

It is appropriate that the levels of need shift and change; it would be inappropriate for individuals to experience a dramatic change and not have their world turned upside down. In these major life changes the individual will experience needs (and a necessity to fulfill those needs) that may have been secondary for a long time.

Third, as the needs of one level are met, the next level above assumes increased importance and dominance. As an individual has enough food, clothing, and shelter to survive in this world, the security needs of that individual will become dominant. As security needs are met, the need for belonging, for relationships with other people, becomes dominant. The individual whose needs for relationships are sufficiently satisfied will experience the primary drive for recognition and esteem. Subsequent to this level, and at the top of the pyramid, is that area of human need for accomplishment and self-fullfillment.

It is as though we move up the pyramid of need one step at a time. The drive to maintain the needs of each level remains with us. But as we fulfill the set of needs at one level, we are then motivated toward the fulfillment of the next. The accomplishment of one level leads to the next. It is true that the steps behind it, the level we have already achieved, will become shaky and at times disappear. We then pay more attention to that shaky level where these needs reassert themselves. It is important to keep in mind that this representation of human need and human motivation is not a picture of "sick" people; it is one way of describing those general themes experienced by all human beings. It is one way of representing what goes on in the life of your neighbor.

Our experience at St. Mary's is that most people are living at the third level. The need for friendship, for belonging, for experiencing love is a very strong, driving force. We believe these needs are only partially and inadequately met for most people. We first began to observe this dynamic in the lives of our patients, their families, and their friends. It became clear that, whatever else was going on in those patient's lives, they were living without the benefit of close personal friendships or love relationships. This was true whether we looked at husbands and wives, parents and children, or "best friend" relationships. There existed within the individual a sense of loneliness and alienation from the world in general and from people with whom they supposedly had close relationships.

Because this sense of loneliness and isolation was an ever present condition of all our patients, it became a matter of intense study, research, and treatment. We wanted to determine the ways in which we could assist the individual to learn how to establish close, intimate, meaningful relationships with other human beings as a way to overcome the sense of loneliness and isolation. Our research and investigation took us outside the patient population. We wanted to find out how other people managed their lives so that loneliness and isolation was not a constant factor.

What we discovered was that a sense of loneliness and isolation appeared in the public at large; it was not a problem unique to chemically dependent people. As our research and investigation continue, the indicators have continued to tell us the same thing. We believe the evidence indicates that a large percentage of our population lives without close intimate relationships. The need is present, the search is present, but somehow, for a large portion of our population, the experience is not present.

We need to examine human relationships to have some way of talking about healthy, stable relationships that are productive and supportive to mental health. Consider the chart in Figure 3, which is part of the work of Dr. John Brantner of the University of Minnesota:

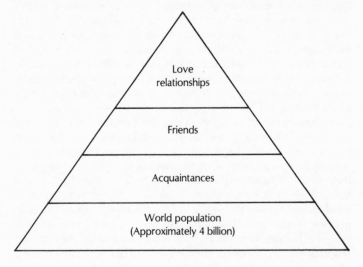

Figure 3

We are social creatures. We need relationships with other people. Out of a world population of approximately four billion people, we meet people, we are introduced to people, we work with people, who become acquantances. We get to know their names and a little about their lives, but the interchange remains fairly superficial. These are the people we know at parties, work, school. We say hello, we converse for a while, we say goodbye. These are not people we know very deeply, and they know little about us. Sharing feelings, such as happiness or pain, tends not to occur with our acquaintances.

Out of all our acquaintances, we begin to select those whom we would like to know better. We are into the process of developing friendships. What we can give and what we can receive begins to deepen with these friends. Our hopes for a deep friendship, our expectation of what that can mean for us, becomes a part of the dynamic. These are the people with whom we want to spend our time. These are the people we will intentionally seek out to share our happiness. These are the people with whom we hope we can share our pain and discomfort. Relationships with our friends move us far beyond the level of acquaintance. Because we are social beings, we need to be with people; but further than that, we need to be with people who will share our experiences.

Just as our friends have developed from our acquaintances, so will love relationships develop from friendships. Out of the population of our several friends, we come to know those people with whom a deeper relationship might be possible. In this relationship, the emotional interchange becomes even more intense. The caring, the giving and receiving take on added importance. Here is a person with whom we can really share the fullness of our lives. We can talk about our deepest pain and our greatest joys. We live with the knowledge that the other person will not reject us but will in fact care for us all the more.

As social creatures, we have built within us the need for close intimate relationships. Our health depends upon it and, in fact, demands it. The drive to develop friends from within our acquaintances, and love relationships from our circle of friends, is as much a part of being a human being as are the needs for food and rest. Most people are constantly searching, constantly attempting to develop more meaningful friendships and deeper love relationships.

This need for intimate relationships is true of the general population, and it relates directly to the chemically dependent person. A person suffering from chemical dependency loses the capability to form and sustain meaningful friendships. As the process of chemical dependency increases, the individual becomes less and less capable of sustaining healthy relationships. The individual will experience increasing loneliness, isolation, and alienation.

Loneliness becomes a way of life. As the pain of loneliness increases, the chemically dependent person relies more and more heavily on the use of mood-altering substances to soften and modify the loneliness and isolation. Whereas the healthy person will depend upon intimate relationships with others to cope with emotional pain, the chemically dependent person will rely primarily on chemicals. The chemically dependent person experiences a primary relationship with chemicals not with other human beings.

4 Peer Pressure and Chemical Dependency

Glen: *Nineteen years old, single:*

I started drinking alcohol and smoking marijuana when I was twelve. I wasn't doing either to excess, but that's when I started. Once I entered high school, drugs really entered my life. I met a lot of people and, of course, in high school friends are really important. I wanted to be liked. I guess I was willing to do whatever I had to do to make and keep friends.

A lot of my friends used drugs, and, as I met more and more people, I tried different types of drugs. And I liked them, I liked feeling high.

I kept my grades up at the beginning. Using drugs didn't seem to bother me, and I didn't believe all the things people were saying about dangers and risks. As time went on, though, I was smoking and drinking more and more. I've always looked older than I really am, so I never had any trouble buying liquor. I was regularly in bars by the time I was seventeen.

That's when things started to change in my life. I lost interest in school. I was always trying to short-cut; I'd skip class and go get high on marijuana. I'd leave home in the morning and not even show up at school if there was going to be a good party that day.

My life was centering around drugs, but at the time I didn't really notice it. As my own drug usage increased, it seemed normal, because all my friends were doing the same thing. I smoked more and

24

more, and soon I was smoking almost constantly. I couldn't even go
to sleep at night without smoking some marijuana.

I was involved in a motorcycle accident not more than ten minutes
after a friend and I had gotten high. At the time I didn't think it could
have possibly had anything to do with drugs. I nearly died in the
accident. We had been trail riding. We stopped, just sat on our bikes
and smoked two or three joints. When we finished we started home.
My friend was far ahead of me when I hit a bad bump, fell and
shoved the handlebars through my ribs. I injured both kidneys and
was bleeding internally. I was knocked unconscious. The accident
happened at about 2:00 in the afternoon. When I awoke, it was
getting dark. I couldn't move my arms or legs; I thought I'd broken my
back. Finally some people came along and took me to a hospital.
Fortunately I have recovered without any disability.

Last year I got a job with a concrete company. The job involved
using a lot of heavy machinery and gave me a lot of responsibility. I
promised myself that I wouldn't get high, that I was going to stay
straight on the job. My drinking and smoking was for the weekends.
But one day an old buddy came by, and I took a couple of hours off.
We went out and smoked so that I was high when I got back to
work. Immediately afterward I messed up with the machine and
dropped a heavy piece of cement on my head. I was in traction for
three weeks with fractured vertebrae. Again, I didn't think smoking
pot had anything to do with my accident. Even while I was in the
hospital, my friends were sneaking me beer and marijuana. I stayed
high half of the time.

When I got out of the hospital, I couldn't go back to work, I was
still recovering from the neck injury. This meant I had a lot of time on
my hands. This is when I really started using alcohol and marijuana
heavily. Every morning the first thing I would do was light up a joint.
Then I'd go out and see some friends. We would bum around all day
and by mid-afternoon would be heavy into our beer drinking. Every
night we were in a bar. I spend every cent I had on drugs.

Finally my Workman's Compensation ran out; the doctor said I was
back to good health and could return to work. But I had no plans of
going back to work. I was having too much fun, getting high, getting
drunk, going to all the parties. I had absolutely no plans for the future,
except to have more fun tomorrow. I didn't know what I was going
to do for money, but I didn't care and I didn't worry about it.

I had a car that was worth quite a bit of money. I really cherished it.
But it was always second on my list. Drugs were always my first.

Finally my life came to a sudden stop. I was out at a party and had my car out there. It was the same scene as always before, the same people I had been hanging around with. I had a few beers out of a keg and brought a few beers of my own, and the party started to break up and everyone was going home to shower and come right back to party some more. As I was driving home, I came around a bend and a car was cutting the curve a little bit and forced me into the ditch. I went back up onto the road and into a tree. That's really the crisis that made me stop and think, because at that point in time I had absolutely no money in my wallet, none in the bank. I kept telling myself "I'm in a pinch, yeah, but I'll get out of it somehow, maybe land a big drug deal or win first place at the Sweepstakes." I had myself talked into it. I knew I didn't want to go back to work. I had no plans. I couldn't hold down a job. When I smashed up my car, it just seemed like my life went right down the drain. The car was the only thing I had left, and now it was gone.

A friend of mine came out and picked me up. She's an older lady. I grew up in the neighborhood with her sons, and both of her sons had quite a bit of trouble with drugs, and they'd gone to a couple of different treatment places. I could see that happening to them, but I never thought of it in terms of myself. I always thought, "That's them, not me. I can handle it. I can maintain. I can get high and get drunk and do all this and still lead a normal life." So I thought. But, suddenly, it was like a big slap in the face. I had nothing. I was rock bottom. There was no way out. There was just no way out this time. My parents had already told me they wouldn't help me financially. I had hit the bottom.

This friend of mine who had come out to pick me up said she wanted to talk to me, but she didn't want to talk to me then because I was drunk. I was high, I was mad and hurt and depressed and I was full of self-pity. She said, "I don't want to talk to you now, but you owe me, so you come over tomorrow when you're sober." I went home that night. I watched them bring my car into the driveway with the tow truck. They threw my bumper on the lawn and then they took off. I looked at it for a minute, went in the house with tears in my eyes. I went straight downstairs, grabbed my pipe and my pot and I got stoned until I didn't know up from down. I smoked myself to sleep.

The next morning I showered and got a call from the neighbor just before I was going to get high. She said, "Are you straight?" I said, "Yeah." She said, "Come on up." So I went over, and for the first time in seven years, I actually sat down with someone and talked about my situation, without getting high, without getting drunk. We sat there and talked. Everything was out in the open. We laid it on the line; tried to find out where I had been going, where I was at at this point, and what could be done about it. She never once suggested anything to me. She never tried to tell me anything about myself. She just seemed to know the right questions to ask for me to bring out everything in myself, and it was very scary. I was looking in the mirror and I didn't like what I saw. I'd been out of school for two years. All my other friends — all my other friends who didn't smoke — were already getting out of college, getting out of school, had steady jobs, and had money in the bank; they seemed to have things going for them, and I had nothing. I had no money. I didn't even have any pot. I said, "Gee, that's not me." Because I know when I think back before I started getting high, I always seemed to get along with teachers and make friends easily. When I thought about it, I decided I just don't need these kinds of problems. It's scary to think that my head had been in the clouds for that long and that life could just pass me by and I didn't even know it. When you finally tell yourself, "You're an alcoholic, you are chemically dependent," it's hard and it hurts.

Starting over from day one when you're twenty years old is pretty ridiculous. I wanted to know what I could do about it. I knew I couldn't quit by myself. I had absolutely no support system. There was no one I could talk to. I couldn't talk to my parents. I couldn't talk to any of my friends. At that point I felt like quitting, but I knew deep in my heart that I could probably quit for a day, maybe two, maybe a week, but that probably would have been it, and then I would have been in the same damned rut as I was before.

The bottom just fell out and there I was, all by myself. So, she said, "You're right, you can't do it by yourself. You're absolutely right, you have to have help." She told me about St. Mary's. She had some literature on it. I read it over and we talked. Both of her boys were getting better. I saw both of their lives go down the drain without realizing that it could have been me I was looking at just as easily. Her sons went through treatment, and they did recover. They didn't have to drink, they didn't have to smoke anymore. They could lead normal productive lives without drugs or alcohol, and I saw how happy they were — just unbelievable. You could just sense it from across the room. When they were doing drugs, in debt, and didn't know where to turn, you could look across the room and tell they were unhappy, you could tell that they didn't know where they were going. They didn't know what was going on, and it was just the opposite when I saw them when they were straight.

Her son came over to my house. He was straight, and he was radiating a glow of happiness. He seemed to know what was going on, he seemed to know where he was going and felt generally good about life. It really made me think. He said, "St. Mary's would be the best, but you know there's no way they're going to be able to help you if you don't want the help. If you're not ready, it's just going to be a waste of everyone's time."

When I smashed up my car, I didn't even think anything that could have happened to me would have been worse than that. After talking and after looking things over, it didn't look so bad anymore. It looked more like a God-send. Things were falling in place for me, and from that point on I had a totally different attitude, even before I came into St. Mary's. I wanted to come in. I really wanted things to work out.

As individuals, we learn not only from our parents, our early childhood experiences, and our continuing associates, we also learn well the lessons of our society. It should be no great surprise to understand that our society places a very positive value on the use of mood-altering chemicals. Most of us grew up in homes where mood-altering chemicals were used daily. And most of us use mood-altering chemicals daily. We receive our caffeine from coffee, tea, chocolate, and cola soft drinks. Caffeine is a very powerful stimulant, and we may self-consciously use it for that purpose. It helps us to get going in the morning: "It really picks me up to have a cup of coffee." The Surgeon General's office reports more people are using more and more tobacco. The nicotine in tobacco is a very powerful stimulant. Alcoholic beverages are drunk in the majority of homes. Alcohol is a very effective sedative. As a sedative, it helps to "take the edge off."

Within our society, there are very strong messages communicated about the use of alcoholic beverages. Traditionally, the drinking of alcohol has been tied to perceptions of masculinity. "I'll meet the boys for a drink after work." The capacity for consumption is perceived as a measure of manhood: "He can hold more liquor than anybody else I know." Sometimes the consumption of alcohol is used as a sign of maturity. Our society has developed transition rites for the passage from childhood to adulthood, and chemicals are the sacrament and sign of that passage. "How much I drink is an indication of my being an adult." The consumption of alcoholic beverages is sometimes associated with increased sophistication. To be a sophisticated human being means to be able to distinguish between various alcoholic beverages, to be able to ask for the right drink, to know when to ask for the right beer, the right wine, or the right mixed drink.

These same dynamics are also true for women. Laws and social customs have changed, and women as well as men are now encouraged to participate in the game of pseudo-sophistication. "It is important to be able to drink." "It is important to be able to drink like the guys." The rate of alcoholism among women is rising, and if it does not yet equal the rate among men, it soon will.

The consumption of alcoholic beverages is also falsely correlated with both physical and mental health. The strong societal message is that something is wrong with the individual who elects not to drink. These attitudes, passed from one person to another and from one generation to another, have all the reinforcement they need from liquor advertising. Such ads will never tell you what the beverage will do for your central nervous system or your coping skills. They usually always portray a combination of sophistication, status, wealth, and friendship, as well as the perennial pose of a good-looking man or woman. We learn our lessons in this society, and we spend our money on those products that offer us what we desire.

There is another very strong dynamic that teaches and continues to reinforce the use of mood-altering chemicals. There is a philosophy in our society that there is a chemical to solve every problem. By and large, we are a people who do not want to deal with pain, discomfort, and loss. This dynamic is manifested in a variety of ways.

People select physicians on the basis of how well a physician will alleviate pain and discomfort; it is as though pain relief is an American right. Rather than dealing with pain and discomfort as evidence of something wrong in the body, all too many people want the symptoms removed immediately; and when the symptoms disappear through the use of pain-killing chemicals, the physician is judged "good." If the physician won't prescribe medication to immediately relieve pain, then that physician is judged "bad." The judgment all too often depends on the physician's ability to alleviate pain not on the physician's ability to correctly identify and treat the cause of the pain.

Check the medicine cabinet of most homes and you will discover an inordinate number of chemicals for relief of pain. However, these chemicals are not only for physical pain; prevalent also will be prescriptive chemicals for emotional pain. The minor tranquilizers have become an American substitute for coping with emotional pain and stress. The very strong message is, "There is a chemical you can take that will make you feel better."

Another major force in our society is the pressure to never show emotion, to mask feelings, and to remain objective. Unfortunately, a large portion of our population believes this is an appropriate way to behave. They believe that to show emotions, to express your feelings, is to be somehow less than mature. It comes with the message presented to children: "Big people don't cry," or "Grin and bear it."

One of the major causes of deteriorating mental health is the inability to express feelings and to give direct expression to emotions. Somehow people begin to believe the erroneous notion that feelings have to be masked, that they should never be expressed, and that people always must present a put-together image. If people operate with this set of attitudes, it will not be long before they begin to experience emotional dysfunction with a variety of manifestations, two of which are loneliness and a sense of isolation.

One of the strong indicators of chemical dependency is the inability to experience and express a wide range of emotions. Mood-altering chemicals mask and cover feeling states. The person who uses mood-altering chemicals will be incapable of recognizing how he or she is feeling. Such individuals are experiencing feelings induced by chemicals rather than those that result from day-to-day living.

Self-alienation is one of the major problems arising from chemical dependency. The chemically dependent person will undergo a deterioration of the ability to distinguish feelings and moods. If left untreated, chemical dependency will ultimately result in a general state of depression and despair. Long before the deterioration gets to this point, however, the individual will gradually lose the ability to experience "normal" feeling states. Most people can differentiate between anger, hurt, disgust, or the feelings that arise from unpleasant situations. Most people experience euphoria, mild pleasure, happiness, and other feelings that result from very pleasant experiences. Chemically dependent people will experience more and more difficulty in truly understanding how they are feeling. This sense of self-alienation becomes more and more destructive.

As all pleasant feelings are stripped away and only negative or painful feelings remain, the individual must find ways to escape and to provide relief from these negative emotional states. As it turns out, the chemicals used to provide relief contribute to a sense of self-alienation, and as alienation increases, relief from intolerable anxieties and emotional symptoms eventually becomes the all-consuming drive of the individual.

Keep in mind that people use mood-altering chemicals for very specific purposes and reasons. Mood-altering chemicals are used to tone down, to modify, to soften the current perception of reality for the individual. The usage may be simply to relax after a hard day's work or to modify the amount of stress an individual is experiencing. It may be to soften the shock and trauma of a very painful experience such as the death of a significant friend or spouse. Chemical usage may be the way a person copes with a very lonely existence.

Whatever the reason, and reasons will vary from individual to individual, a certain grouping of chemicals are chosen because those chemicals do effectively modify and soften perceived pain. We all have the experience of using chemicals to dull the perception of physical pain. The use of aspirin compound, for example, is widespread. We suffer mentally, emotionally, and spiritually as well as with our physical bodies. Mood-altering chemicals are just as effective in softening emotional pain as they are in reducing the pain of a toothache. Mood-altering chemicals will be just as effective in temporarily reducing mental anguish as a ''pain killer'' is for a severe headache. Let us turn next to an examination of the kinds of chemicals that will effectively modify and change our perception of reality.

5 Commonly Used Chemicals and Chemical Dependency

In the long list of chemicals, either natural or manufactured, there is a small number of chemicals that modify our perception of reality. Of all the chemicals known today, only a relatively few are capable of creating dependency and addiction within human beings. Interestingly enough, the only chemicals capable of producing chemical dependency and addiction are the chemicals that will alter and change our moods and our perception of reality.

You can drink all the orange juice you want and never become addicted; it will not alter your perception of reality. But if you start drinking coffee, you are dealing with a very powerful chemical that can effectively alter and change how you feel and how you perceive the world. The potential for effecting mood and perception exists within the chemical. The most commonly used mood-altering chemicals today are:

Alcohol	Codeine	Marijuana	Sleeping pills
Amphetamines	Darvon	Morphine	Talwin
Barbiturates	Demerol	Nicotine	Tranquilizers
Caffeine	Hashish	Opium	(minor)
Cocaine	Heroin	Percodan	

Approximately 85 percent of the American population are chemical users on a regular basis. Certainly, not all usage is harmful, nor is it always detrimental to physical or mental health. There are three major categories or classifications of drug use that need to be kept in mind. Each category is different from the others, and we ought not to lump all people who use chemicals into a single grouping.

First, there are healthy, "normal" people who use mood-altering chemicals from the list above and do not experience damage to themselves, they do not experience a diminishing of their capability, nor do they experience emotional or physical illness as a result of their chemical usage. These individuals will be selective as to the type of chemical, when it is used, under what circumstances, and the size of dosage. They will use the chemical to achieve a desired effect and then stop.

Second, there is a group of individuals who occasionally abuse one or more of the mood-altering chemicals and experience some detrimental effect from the use. These detrimental effects may be emotional, social, intellectual, spiritual, or physical. This may be the type of person who will depend upon the chemical to continually reduce anxiety and tension. Individuals within this category are not exhibiting demonstrable physical addiction, but they are experiencing the early dynamics of chemical dependency. This is an emotional dependency that has not yet reached a demonstrable physical level.

The third category of drug users are those whose dependency has now reached a physical level through their continued use of one or more of the mood-altering chemicals. Individuals within this category suffer emotional, social, intellectual, spiritual, and physical consequences. We estimate that 10 to 15 percent of the general population either are or will become addicted to mood-altering substances.

Just how dangerous are these chemicals? How potent are they? What risks do we run in using them? Three observations need to be made considering human beings and this list of chemicals.

First of all, through laboratory tests and experimentation, we know that human beings are more susceptible to chemical dependency than are other mammals. It is easier to effect addiction in a human being than in a monkey, for example. The higher up the animal chain, the easier it is to become dependent.

Second, it is possible to induce dependency in animals, including human beings, with every one of the mood-altering chemicals listed above.

Third, in every one of these substances, there is an index of addiction. Each of these substances can be ranked according to their potential for creating addiction.

Through research, it is also possible to rank each of these chemicals

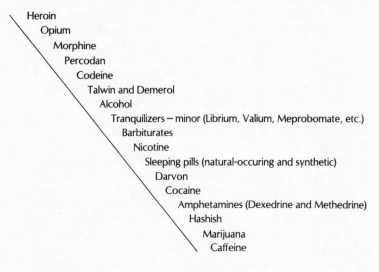

Figure 4

according to their potential for creating dependency (see Figure 4). The higher a substance appears on the chart, the greater potential it has for creating dependency. For example, we can predict that, if someone regularly uses heroin, his or her chances of becoming dependent approach 100 percent. At the other end of the scale, there is a substantial reduction in the index of dependency, but even with regular use of caffeine there is a significant degree of dependency.

Three additional comments need to be made about this index of dependency.

First, if we remove amphetamines, cocaine, caffeine, and nicotine from the list, all the remaining substances are anxiety reducing — their major use is to reduce the level of anxiety experienced by the individual.

Second, these chemicals are very predictable and effective. Their effect can be very immediate, and the individual will experience a reduction in the level of anxiety.

Third, the effect of the chemical on the body is paradoxical. Initially, each chemical will reduce the level of anxiety within the individual.

Eventually, however, there is a second effect upon the body. The individual not only will experience the return of anxiety, but will in fact experience more anxiety than before the chemical was used. These chemicals are *biphasic,* meaning that they will both reduce anxiety and, in a delayed effect, increase anxiety.

All of these mood-altering substances share a common pattern in the development of chemical dependency. That pattern is specific — by this I mean it can be described. That pattern is universal — by this I mean it will always be present in chemical dependency. Regardless of the individual and regardless of the chosen chemical, the dynamics of dependency are the same. The following example uses alcohol as the drug of choice. The example could just as well be that of amphetamines, tranquilizers or heroin.

How is it that an individual can become chemically dependent with alcohol? To put it in more common terms, how does somebody become an alcoholic?

The answer to the question has to do with both individual personality and the effects of alcohol on the body. As discussed earlier, everyone has coping abilities developed at varying levels of sophistication. For some, this means that coping abilities are underdeveloped; they have never really developed the skills necessary to manage in the face of conflict, anxiety, and pain. What might seem a minor problem for one of us might be major for another. Some people have aged without developing a reservoir of coping skills. Others, having a reservoir of coping skills, will run into situations beyond their ability to manage and cope.

When life becomes too stressful, when our level of tolerance for stress is reached, our coping mechanisms break down, and each of us will behave in ways to dull the perception of the stress. Both the individual whose coping devices are underdeveloped and someone with a fairly sophisticated set of coping skills face a degree of stress for which there is no internal compensation.

Of all the devices known for altering perceptions of reality, the most easily available and the most effective is the use of mood-altering chemicals, called *psychotropic drugs.* They alter the mood or consciousness of the individual. These chemicals are effective in altering reality because they have only one major site of action in the body — they directly affect the central nervous system (CNS). Specifically, three parts of the CNS are affected by psychotropic drugs: the cerebral cortex, the limbic system, and the medulla (see Figure 5).

Perception or awareness of reality is achieved through that part of

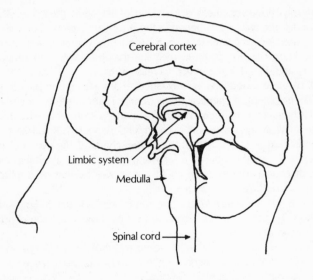

Figure 5

the CNS known as the *cerebral cortex.* This part of the brain has very specific functions in its normal operating state. It is the site for rational thought, integration of memory, the understanding of abstract concepts, fine motor coordination, perception of time, problem-solving capabilities, and data retrieval (memory). It is the site of awareness for what is going on around us, and it is with this part of the brain that we rationally respond to the world around us. This is the site of intellectual processes in the human being.

The *limbic system* (part of the mid-brain) controls our mood state. Out of the limbic system comes our depression or our excitement; our mood in response to reality.

The *medulla,* located where the brain is attached to the spinal cord, controls basic body functions such as regularity of the heart, blood pressure, body temperature, and rate of breathing.

Psychotropic drugs affect the functioning of these three specific parts of the brain in the above order—first the cerebral cortex, second the limbic system, and finally the medulla. It is as though each of these three parts of the brain have their own tolerance level or degree to which they are sensitive to the drug. A small dose of a psychotropic drug will have a greater effect on the limbic system than it does on the medulla. Or it may have little or no effect on the medulla, but it will effect the cerebral cortex. The individual will experience decreased ability to perform fine motor coordination, perception of time may be slightly distorted, abstract thinking and problem solving will become confused, and rational thought will be dulled.

There is also a very specific relationship between the size of the dose, the frequency of use, and the degree of dysfunction within these three parts of the brain. As the dosage increases, so will the degree of dysfunction.

Regardless of the reasons given by an individual, psychotropic chemicals are used for their effect on the central nervous system. "It makes me feel better." "I really like the way I feel now." These drugs work, and they work because they affect the very parts of the brain that control our perception of reality and how we feel about it. Psychotropic drugs are used to alter the basic perception of reality.

Most people are constantly aware of at least some degree of internal stress. This stress may result from their work, their home life, their interpersonal relationships, or perhaps even a mild dissatisfaction with who they are and what they are doing with their lives. Awareness of this pervasive, low-grade stress can be altered by the use of chemicals. The chemical action within the body is consistent and predictable, and if you can control the dosage, you can obtain a predictable mood level. There is a chemical term that is appropriate here: *titration*. Titration simply means that you can learn to mix a number of chemicals to reach a predetermined end-point. People learn to titrate, to juggle a mixture of chemicals, in order to get to a predetermined mood. Most people who consume alcoholic beverages learn this lesson very quickly. People learn fairly quickly the effect of one or two drinks, how much they can drink before they get sick, and how much they can drink before they will experience a hangover the next day.

Psychotropic drugs are toxic to the CNS. Alcohol intoxication is basically a state of toxicity within the CNS. The CNS cannot respond in its normal functioning capacity; a toxic state has been introduced that impairs its function. This is potentially true of all psychotropic drugs. The process is the same whether it is a legal or illegal psychotropic drug, whether it is alcohol or a prescription from your physician. If you medicate to alter perceptions of pain, tension, and stress, you do this by creating a state of toxicity within the CNS to achieve reduction of pain, tension, and stress.

Some psychotropic drugs are used in the treatment of mental disorders. For instance, if a person suffering a major psychosis uses prescriptive psychotropic chemicals, the purpose and the effect is to move the brain to a more normal state of functioning. In major psychosis, the brain is chemically imbalanced, and with the use of psychotropic drugs, the balance can be restored. The treatment of major psychotic states is an appropriate use of these medications, such as control of schizophrenia.

Whether use of the psychotropic drugs is prescribed by a physician for medicinal purposes or it is an individual choice for mood modification, the goal is the same; namely, to alter the state of the CNS sufficiently to achieve a predetermined end result: reduction of pain, tension, or stress. The individual or the physician determines how much of the psychotropic drug should be used. The dosage will allow enough alteration of brain physiology to change the perception of reality, but it will not induce a state of toxicity that renders the individual incapable of functioning. To be drunk is to have enough alcohol in the CNS to create a state of acute toxicity.

The most apparent need of individuals who use psychotropic drugs is to alter the basic functioning of the limbic system, which is responsible for the emotional states we experience. By altering the functioning of the limbic system, the individual can alter his or her basic mood or emotional response to reality. For example, alcohol is a depressant. Why is it that many people experience euphoria, a state of pleasantness, from the consumption of alcohol? If alcohol is a depressant, then why don't people feel depressed when they drink it? Many people experience euphoria because the alcohol alters the levels of anxiety and the perceptions of stress, thereby freeing them from these mood states and allowing them to experience euphoria.

As the individual continues to medicate with psychotropic drugs, and the blood levels of the drug increase, the physiological effect will move down the brain stem from the cerebral cortex, through the limbic system, to the medulla. This advance of toxicity into the medulla occurs in advanced states of intoxication. When this occurs, the individual is in a critical medical state because the medulla controls the respiratory rate and heartbeat. An overdose of a psychotropic drug can result in the chemical depression of the medulla. Most people do not use psychotropic drugs to this point. Acute toxic depression of the medulla can also occur with large numbers of the mood-altering chemicals.

In our society, a phenomenon has occurred recently to add even further risk to the use of psychotropic drugs. This phenomenon is poly-drug use. Quite simply, this means that people are using a combination of drugs rather than a single chemical. In part, this has occurred because of the increased manufacturing of psychotropic chemicals for use in prescription. Because these drugs are such effective mood modifiers, physicians prescribe them for the control of anxiety, the reduction of symptoms, the control of depression, and the control of sleep.

Only recently has the medical profession come to understand the effect of these drugs within a person who is also consuming alcohol. For example, the combined use of alcohol and tranquilizers has a synergistic effect within the CNS. That is, one dose of alcohol and one dose of a tranquilizer do not equal two doses of a sedative; taken in combination they equal not two but perhaps twenty or thirty alcohol-tranquilizer doses. This exponential effect accounts for a much higher rate of drug overdose among people who are poly-drug users.

Poly-drug use is not limited to alcohol and tranquilizers. All people should be extremely careful if they are going to use more than one psychotropic drug. However, in poly-drug use alcohol is almost always one of the combined drugs. Whatever else people are using, they will probably be drinking alcohol. Alcohol is by far the most commonly consumed drug in our society. In terms of sheer numbers of people using drugs, alcohol must be rated number one. It is the easiest to acquire. It is the drug most endorsed by our society. Because of its effectiveness, it is the major drug of choice. It is so commonly accepted that it is the number-one social drug. While all of these facts are true, and while it is true that most people who consume alcoholic beverages do not become alcoholics, we need to remember that alcohol is a psychotropic drug. It acts upon the CNS just like any other psychotropic drug.

We are living in a world of shifting drug use. There is a steady increase in the number of people who come into treatment because of poly-drug addiction. We are seeing many people in treatment as a result of the combined use of marijuana and alcohol. Because alcohol is so readily available, and because it is so effective, people quickly learn how to temporarily alter their perception of reality. The consumption of alcohol and the learning of "how much you need to feel good" becomes an operative coping mechanism.

Consider for a moment the adolescent dealing with the inevitable pain associated with growing up. In order to successfully work through the continuing development of self-identity, in order to successfully experience the development of interpersonal friendships, in order to refine and give expression to a personal value system, adolescents must experience emotional pain. To come out on the other side of that personal strife and pain as healthy, productive human beings, adolescents must learn to cope with a painful reality, and their tolerance of pain must be increased. If this can be accomplished, they will realize a better sense of self-adequacy, will have increased the ability to relate to others, and will have ways to adequately cope with anxiety and depression.

However, if a mood-altering chemical is introduced into this process, if alcohol or marijuana becomes a part of coping with the pain of reality, then adolescents learn something far different — they learn that a chemical can make them feel better. They come away with a false sense of adequacy, deluded in the ability to relate to other people. They experience a temporary lessening of anxiety and depression, a temporary mood shift toward euphoria and pleasantness.

Once this learning occurs, the use of alcohol or any other mood-altering chemical becomes a way of coping. The learning tends to become permanent. Coping with reality in this way becomes the pattern. This pattern increases the learning in how to get the desired results from mood-altering chemicals.

This dynamic of learning is certainly not exclusively limited to adolescence. Any individual can learn this. All that is needed is for the individual to experience a situation where reality has become too harsh and too stressful.

Tranquilizers, marijuana, and alcohol are the most widely used forms of medication for reducing the pain of stress. If the individual continues to medicate stress, without at the same time learning new ways to cope with stress, in all likelihood that individual will live the rest of his or her life using medication as a way to cope.

6 Stress, Loneliness, and Chemical Dependency

Clarke: *thirty-seven years old, divorced:*

I come from an alcoholic home. My father was an alcoholic. I remember going down to the bars when he was bartending. In the wintertime we'd have to haul him home in a sled; in the summertime, in a wagon. This continued until I was eight years old. At this time my father disappeared for a couple of days. He came back and he never touched liquor after that. He joined AA to be reinforced. He never told anyone where he went for those two days, but he never touched another drop for the rest of his life.

That first eight years made an impression on me, and that's why I didn't start drinking in high school. Also, I was very church-conscious. I had a relationship with my God. I accepted the Lord, Jesus Christ, in high school. I was president of our youth group, and I was president of the choir. After high school I went to college, and all of a sudden, things were different. I wasn't popular. There were people from all over, and it frightened me. When I entered college, I was thinking about going into the ministry. I was there one year, and the pressure of not being popular, of not really knowing what I wanted then, well, I dropped out and joined the Navy.

In November of 1960 was the first time I got drunk. I had just finished boot camp. I had checked into my next duty station. I got into a group where I was just typing records and doing general work. Some buddies and I started into Chicago on the liberty weekend. We

41

*were drinking in the car on our way. This was my first real experience
with liquor. We'd pass it around and I'd take my shot. I remember we
had to stop somewhere by Lake Michigan and I got out of the car. I
was on my knees and I couldn't walk. . When we got into Chicago, I
remembered seeing the skyline, but I didn't know where we were.*

*On the way back to base, I passed out. I got up the next morning,
but I couldn't eat and I got sick. I just sat on the floor with my head on
the toilet. I just couldn't believe how bad I felt. After that I don't
remember getting into drinking sprees. I just got turned off from
alcohol, and for three years I didn't drink.*

*I was transferred to an air station near my folks, and I really
behaved. I took care of them. I met my future wife at this time also.
She was actually my high school sweetheart, but when I joined the
Navy we lost touch. I was transferred back, and we got back
together again. She really made an impression on my dad and on my
mother. They always wanted us to get married. We went to our
minister to take some tests, and I lied on parts of the test so it would
look like we were compatible. My folks were very, very happy, and
all the relatives thought it was the greatest thing that could ever
happen, and yet, in the back of my mind I was afraid. But we were
going to get married.*

*At the bachelor's party, I got totally drunk. We were at the Enlisted
Men's Club at the Naval Air Station. I was drinking sloe gin fizzes. I can
remember that because I was bragging. I thought they tasted just like
cherry pop. We were playing a game and if you lost, you'd have to
drink your drink. I found out later that the main purpose of the game
was to get me drunk. So I drank an awfully lot. Later I got in my car
and headed home.*

*I stopped at my fiancee's house. She was living at home at the time.
I made a complete ass out of myself. It was the first time that she had
seen me drunk. I went up into the house, fell on the porch, got up,
straightened myself out and rang the doorbell. She and her mother
came to the door, and I told her I wanted my ring back. She started
crying. Her mother started crying. She said, "You go home and talk to
your mother and then call me back when you're sober."*

*At the time I didn't know how much this was going to be thrown
into my face later on. But anyway I went home. My folks had never
seen me drunk. My sister and brother had never seen me drunk — I
had never been drunk at home. I went into the bathroom and
proceeded to get sick. My sister, thinking I had the flu, called my*

mother. She walked in the door, looked at me on the bathroom floor, and knew right away that I was drunk. She was very disgusted. All of a sudden, memories of my dad were flashing back.

I made some promises to my mom and my fiancee. Thery were all worried that I was going to turn out like my dad. Whenever this was brought up, I hated it. I especially hated it from my fiancee because she had never seen my dad drunk. It was just what she had heard, and I resented her for that.

But we went ahead and got married. We had a mutual agreement that I was going to go back to school. I was going into either teaching or the ministry. At that time I had lost touch with God again. I hadn't been going to church while in the Navy, and that bothered me. When I got married I got very involved in our church again. I was a deacon and the secretary of the church. I was happy. I was going to school, I was into something. I was back into the church and people were saying they could see how happy I was. I loved working with the youth and just being involved with the church.

We had made an agreement as far as children because we both had a feeling that we had to give ourselves time to know each other and we didn't want children right away. We were married in February and a daughter was born in November. When my wife told me she was pregnant, I said, "Why? How? What happened? I thought you were on the pill?" She said, "No, the only way I could hold on to you was to have a child." She knew that I just went crazy over kids. I just loved them.

So our daughter was born during the time I was going to school. I was driving an ambulance. I lied to my wife a couple of times. I told her I was going on an ambulance run, but I would go to a bar and have a couple of drinks. Never enough to really get drunk — just getting into the bar. When our daughter was born I was happy. I really was. I had a little girl, but I still had a feeling toward my wife that we never got straightened out. We never went to see anybody. We never went to see our minister. We never brought our problems up to anybody. So, I thought to myself, "I'll really try to make this work for my daughter."

For a couple of years, I didn't drink that much, but I was sneaking some. We had friends I had met in the service and were invited over to their house. We had two or three couples that we were close to, and they always had beer. We never had liquor in the house. But I wanted it so I could offer people beer. I went to the liquor store and bought a case of beer. I brought it back, put it in the refrigerator. I really upset my wife. She just couldn't understand why I had to have that. Our friends came over, and when I offered them a beer they got upset. They said, "We never expected to see liquor; we knew this was one place we could come to and we could have friends without the liquor involvement." That sort of shot me down. It bothered me.

Then I started drinking the beer at home by myself. Everytime I had more than three or four beers in a night my wife would bring it up, "You're drinking too much, you're going to turn out like your dad." This kept bothering me.

I couldn't make it in school. I just didn't feel right again. So I reenlisted in the Navy for two years. I used the excuse that I had to go back in to get myself straightened out. I really knew in the back of my mind that there was room and board if I ever got kicked out of the house. I was drinking more and more but I didn't get drunk for two years — testing myself.

My wife and I had been getting further and further apart. After I got out I didn't go back to school. She wasn't happy at all with me going into business. My boss had a Christmas party and had all the employees to his house. I went through the punch pretty good and had at least twelve bottles of beer. I was thoroughly drunk. I embarrassed the people there. I didn't embarrass my boss because he got drunk first and went upstairs and passed out on the bed. To prove to my wife that I wasn't drunk, I said, "I'll drive." I had to pull over and I threw up all over the car inside. My wife was crying. She said, "Let me drive." I said, "no, it must be something I ate." Keep in mind, she hadn't been close to anyone drinking in her life. This was a Saturday night party. Sunday morning I got up and she said, "Okay, before church, you go out and clean that car." I opened up the car door and I got sick all over again. She went to church with her parents.

Then I started lying to her when I was going out with the people from work. First it was just the Friday night thing and then it would be a couple of nights. I wouldn't get drunk but always had three or four beers.

I started getting further away from the church. She saw this, and it really upset her. Also, there was a conflict in the congregation between the senior pastor and the assistant pastor, and it split the congregation in half. I had been living in a world where I never thought that would happen in a church, and it sort of let me down —

at least that's what I was using. I was feeling bad about what I was doing with my drinking, and I was trying to blame the church.

My wife and I went to a business convention. Of course there was drinking, but I did not get drunk. I was getting used to drinking. I was getting used to the beer, and it was always available. There was no need for me to try and quit. I was drinking three or four or five or six bottles of beer. Not every night, but I was drinking it.

My wife and I started to get further and further apart. We bought a home which she picked out. I was losing interest. I said, "If you want a house, you go and pick one out and we'll get it." So she went out and found one a block from her parents' house. Her parents were very understanding. They would not come over unless they were invited. They would not drop by to see us. They knew something was happening. We weren't communicating. We were fighting. Here, again, it wasn't over getting drunk. It was over the two or three bottles. We separated a year later.

I quit my job because I had an offer from another company as a manager. Still I hadn't really been drunk, but I was doing steady drinking. Friends at the company I was leaving threw a going-away party for me. It was probably one of the few times I was out drinking and I wasn't buying. I cannot remember getting home. It was the first time, and would be far from the last, where I would wake up to see if the car was there. But I drove, and it didn't bother me. I wasn't worried at that time. I thought, "I'd better slow down. I'll watch myself—I won't drink as much."

I started with the company. Everything was going great. I was located downtown. I got started with some of the salesmen and some of the people who had been there a while, and we made a habit of stopping after work and having a few drinks. Here, again, I watched it because I wanted to make a good impression on the new company. I didn't want them to think "Oh boy, we hired a lush." I really wanted to go places with the company. That lasted for about a year. Then the company moved me to another city.

There was a party, and we went out and celebrated. This time I was buying drinks. I started something that was going to follow me all the way through my drinking—buying drinks to try to keep the people going with me.

I got my job going pretty good in the new city. The drinking wasn't interfering with my work. I didn't think I had a drinking problem. But I had a hard time getting to meet people. The only place I would meet people was in bars.

One night after a party I was arrested for drunken driving, a DWI. The company I was trying to put a show on for . . . . all of a sudden, whammo, I thought, "Oh, my God, everything's gone. They're going to have me back home overnight." I called the salesman I had there. I was allowed the one call, and he came down and got me out of the tank after I had my mug shot and my prints taken. I didn't call the home office. I started lying more and more. I didn't want them to know. I thought, "As long as I don't tell them. I'll get the car fixed out of my own pocket." The bill came to $985 for my car. I got that taken care of, and I just thought I'd better get going straight and get my act together. As long as the home office doesn't find out about this DWI and I get the car fixed, and in the back of my mind I kept thinking, "Jesus, I hope they don't drop in on me all of a sudden." You know, a surprise visit from the home office and I've got this banged-up car. So I got it fixed. By now I had met people in the neighborhood bars. I had started spending money I didn't have. I just wanted to buy friendship. I wanted to get out of this loneliness. I wanted people to like me. And what's the easiest way? Buy them a couple of drinks. You'll be their friend as long as you're in that bar. I got to know the owners of the bar. I had forgotten all about church. I forgot about God. I really didn't care what was happening.

No one knew what I was doing down there. I was safe. Out of a five-day work week I would go to work for maybe two days. Otherwise I was drinking. I wasn't enjoying it, but I could forget my loneliness. I didn't bother to get involved in a church. I didn't try to make any other friends but the bar people. They were the easiest people to get to know. I didn't have to be honest with them. They liked me, because I was buying them drinks.

I don't know how the branch office kept going, but it did. It showed some growth. I think part of the reason was when they got rid of the branch manager down there anything was better than he was. The old accounts came back, and I looked good when I first got down there.

I found a bar that opened up at 6:00 in the morning, and I got to know the people real well there. I moved out of the apartment I was living in. I moved in with a guy I met in a bar. I didn't know it at the time, but he was also an alcoholic. I didn't think anything of it. I still didn't have a drinking problem. I was moving in with an alcoholic. I can handle it, I may even be able to help him; this was my reasoning. his bar was always stocked with half-gallons.

Something that was happening with my drinking . . . I would be sitting at bars with other people, and we would be talking about the problems other people we knew had with their drinking. Looking back, it was pathetic. Here we would be sitting getting drunk. I think I could go down there tonight and those same people would be sitting there.

Eventually the company moved me back to its home office, promoted me, and gave me an almost unlimited budget. There was a lot of frustration staying in the home office trying to get the work done. I tried to find a girlfriend. I didn't have anybody and I was feeling embarrassed about trying to find somebody. This frustration just kept coming on and getting harder and harder.

One night three women from the office and I went out drinking after work. We were all drunk. On the spur of the moment I invited them to go to California with me at the company's expense. So, that night we drove to the airport and took off. For three days we drank and partied, all on the company credit cards.

When I returned, I was too afraid to go to the office. I stayed home and refused to answer the phone or the door. Finally I talked to a neighbor, and she started telling about St. Mary's. I got up the courage to talk to the boss, and he agreed to keep me on if I repaid the money and went into treatment; otherwise I was fired.

There are two severely negative consequences to the continued use of mood-altering chemicals as a way of coping with pain and stress. First of all, it is true that the chemical will initially reduce the pain. The individual will experience positive relief from anxiety, a sense of "feeling better." The individual will feel, if not euphoria, at least a reduction in pain. However, this euphoria, this reduction in the level of pain, is only temporary. When the stress returns, the chemical must be used again. The individual has not learned how to increase coping capabilities.

Something else occurs with prolonged use of mood-altering chemicals, something that seems absolutely opposed to the effect of reducing anxiety. If an individual medicates for a long period of time as a way to reduce the level of experienced anxiety, the opposite will eventually begin to occur. An increased level of anxiety will be experienced as a direct result of using a mood-altering chemical. As previously stated, alcohol is a biphasic drug. One of the characteristics of alcohol is that it will chemically lower anxiety only to result, a few hours later, in a chemically induced state of higher anxiety.

An individual uses alcohol to reduce levels of anxiety, but those levels of anxiety become heightened by the use of alcohol. The individual has a choice to make: to consume more alcohol or find other ways of coping with uncomfortable and intolerable levels of anxiety. If the individual chooses the former route and begins to consume just a little bit more alcohol each time to reduce the level of experienced anxiety, then he or she will discover it takes more and more alcohol to produce the same effect. This graduation into a drinking pattern to handle anxiety is not the result of a one-time conscious decision. For most people, this occurs gradually, and over a long period of time.

Recall that one of the characteristics of chemical dependency is its extreme sense of alientation and loneliness. This dynamic of loneliness also occurs during the search for anxiety reduction, as can be seen in Figure 6.

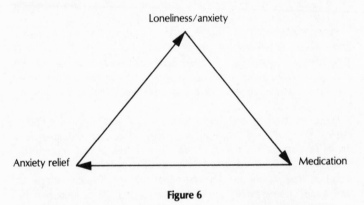

Figure 6

Assume for a moment that an individual experiences loneliness. This is a common feeling. However, suppose the loneliness becomes very painful and does not appear to be temporary but rather is prolonged. This may happen when there is a move to a new city, or perhaps the children have grown and left home, or a spouse has died. In any event, loneliness can become so unbearable that medication is used to dull the senses, to take the edge off the loneliness.

The continued use of psychotropic drugs to reduce anxiety also prevents the development of healthy human relationships. If healthy relationships exist, continued abuse of psychotropic drugs will be destructive of those relationships. Developing and sustaining interpersonal relationships requires the experience of frustration, tension, and emotional pain. If an individual is using chemicals to alleviate those feelings, then the relationships can never fully develop.

Many relationships are initiated within a medicated state. There are many couples whose dating pattern is so interrelated with the use of alcohol or marijuana that they do not have the opportunity to get to know each other in a nonmedicated state. This is a common pattern for many couples. After marriage, the couple needs to continue the medicated relationship in order to sustain the kind of feeling that brought them together in the first place. If use of mood-altering chemicals continues, the usage pattern will lead to chemical dependency of one or both of the partners and may result in the destruction of the marriage.

7 Four Types of Chemically Dependent People

Our experience indicates that there appear to be four distinct types of individuals who encounter chemical dependency as a part of their life. These four groupings are derived from a careful examination of the thousands of people who have been a part of the St. Mary's Treatment Program.

1. Individuals whose major coping mechanism for stress and anxiety is medication. These individuals have limited coping ability and a very low tolerance for stress and emotional pain. Whenever anything begins to go wrong, whenever they begin to perceive pressure, their immediate response is to reduce the tension through medication.

2. Individuals who have developed a fairly adequate set of coping skills. They have productively functioned in their work, in their home, in their interpersonal relationships. Their tolerance to stress, however, is fairly low. As long as life goes fairly smoothly, these individuals have no difficulty in coping. But as stress increases, they reach their limit for coping. The coping mechanisms of these people have been sufficient for most of their lives, but under major life changes the mechanisms are simply not strong enough to handle the stress. If the coping mechanisms are not capable of handling major life changes, and the individual uses mood-altering chemicals to cope with the anxiety and pain, then chemical dependency can easily develop.

3. Individuals whose basal metabolism is different from the average. Some laboratory research indicates that some people are meta-

bolically predisposed to abuse psychotropic drugs. Scientists have identified liver enzymes and brain enzymes in this type of individual that differ from those of the average person.

4. Individuals who are predisposed to chemical dependency due to their heredity. There is some clinical research indicating that some chemically dependent people have a genetic history that predisposes them to increased chances of dependency. There needs to be more research in this area to determine the extent to which heredity plays a determining role. It does appear, however, that some people become chemically dependent not because their drinking patterns are abusive but because of their genetic structure. This type of individual accounts for a very small percentage of the chemically dependent population.

In this typology, the individuals who are metabolically or genetically predisposed to chemical dependency represent a grouping of people for whom chemical dependency is not directly related to their coping skills. They simply cannot consume alcoholic beverages for either pleasure or relaxation. Their physical makeup will not permit it.

By contrast, individuals within the first two classifications are not genetically predisposed to chemical dependency, but they are prime candidates for chemical dependency if their coping skills are not strengthened and reinforced.

As previously described, when an individual consumes an alcoholic beverage, the result is the development of a toxic state within the CNS. When the individual ceases consumption of the alcoholic beverage, the process of detoxification begins. This is a normal biological process by which the body metabolizes the toxic material into harmless substances, which are excreted. When all of the alcohol has left the individual, that individual is the same as he or she was before drinking.

However, if heavy drinking occurs over a period of months or years, significant changes begin to occur. The individual begins to experience significant changes in emotional state, whether he or she is drinking or not. The individual will begin to experience a sense of pervasive anxiety, an edginess about what is going on. The individual will begin to undergo a deepening sense of shame and a deepening sense of guilt. "I know I shouldn't do this, and I feel bad about it."

The individual will become aware of a general sense of anger. The individual won't be able to say specifically what makes him or her angry, because everything does. Anger becomes nonfocused and nonspecific.

Following closely with anger is a growing sense of resentment. The individual begins to resent himself or herself. Ultimately, all of these emotional states lead to an increased sense of alienation, rejection, and loneliness.

As these feelings and emotional states emerge, the individual is motivated to increase the use of alcohol, since the ability to cope with strong negative feelings was limited in the first place. The individual reaches a point where he or she is no longer drinking to get high (to attain a state of euphoria and good feelings) but is now drinking to feel somewhat normal. (For an expanded explanation of this dynamic, the reader is again referred to Johnson's *I'll Quit Tomorrow.*) With more drinking and stronger negative feelings, the individual begins to consider the possibility that he or she is insane; suicide and other destructive behavior will be considered as possible solutions.

At the same time that these significant changes occur in the emotional states of the individual, behavioral changes are also occurring. The individual begins doing and saying things that would not have previously been said or done, for instance, becoming verbally and physically abusive. Painful experiences can result in behavioral changes. People will attempt to resolve and reduce the pain. When the resolution of pain involves the continued use of mood-altering chemicals, the individual will eventually reach the point where the use of chemicals produces additional painful experience, which results in behavioral changes, which results in chemical use — and the cycle is reinforced (see Figure 7).

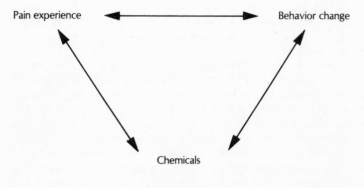

Figure 7

Many people use moderate amounts of alcohol to alleviate feelings of pain, stress, and anxiety. Alcohol is effective; it does modify these feeling states. However, when these emotional pain states rise, again alcohol will be used. If the pain level increases, then more alcohol must be used as medication. Eventually the alcohol will produce a toxic state within the CNS, and the individual's toxic-produced behavior will in and of itself become pain-producing. Medicated behavior is different, entirely different, from the behavior generally associated with that individual. If this medicated behavior is perceived by the individual as "crazy," "bizarre," or "out of the ordinary," then that individual experiences more pain, more anxiety, and will need to use more alcohol in the search for a tolerable perception of reality.

The individual experiences a disintegration of his or her value system and a breakdown of interpersonal relationships. The more behavior changes, the more the person becomes dysfunctional, the more negative impact there is on the feeling state, the more the individual experiences a rapid disintegration of self-worth. Eventually, ego strength will become limited and vulnerable. Ultimately, the individual will come to the point where he or she perceives desolation from within and from without. Hopelessness and despair become the predominant emotional states. The individual experiences alienation and isolation from self, from others, from God.

What causes this downward spiral to occur? Why should the drinking of alcohol result in the disintegration of an individual's personality? Again, the answer has to do with the effect of alcohol on the CNS. With continued heavy use of alcohol, three basic changes occur within the brain:

1. There is a significant reduction of viable, functional cells in the cerebral cortex.

2. As brain cells are injured and die, scar tissue forms around the injured and dying cells.

3. There will be microscopic hemorrhaging of the capillaries supplying blood to the brain.

These physically destructive changes in the brain occur because of two basic physiological facts.

First, the human body has the ability to regenerate body tissues, to heal injuries. This is true with one exception: The tissues of the CNS cannot be regenerated.

Second, human beings are aerobic organisms, which means that our bodies require a constant flow of oxygen to the capillaries to sustain cellular health. If the oxygen flow to any part of the body is diminished, the cells and tissues of that part suffer. The area most sensitive to oxygen deprivation is the CNS.

When an individual uses mood-altering chemicals, predictable results occur in the cellular structure of the blood. Intoxication results in the slowing down of the flow of red cells through the vessels and capillaries. Because the rate of flow has slowed, the red cells form clusters whereas normally they would be evenly distributed. Oxygen is carried by these red cells. Because the rate of flow is slower and because they are clustered the flow of oxygen is disturbed, thereby causing the tissue cells to become oxygen-deficient in a short period of time.

Areas of the CNS, specifically the cerebral cortex, undergo cellular death during periods of intoxication. Once they are destroyed, there is no regeneration. For every period of intoxication, additional cells within the cerebral cortex are damaged and die. Also, when people experience cortical damage in the CNS, it effects them emotionally, socially, intellectually, spiritually, and physically. This damage is added to the already existing emotional and behavioral changes previously mentioned. The individual becomes unwittingly locked in a descending spiral of increasing dysfunction. This dysfunction has its cost in the decreased ability to live, to love, and to work.

According to NIAAA research it is estimated that 50 percent of the drinking population will at some time during their lives experience an abusive drinking pattern, and that 10 to 15 percent of the drinking population will become alcoholics. Our experience at St. Mary's indicates that the number of people abusing psychotropic drugs is increasing, and the projections indicate that the number will greatly add to those already experiencing alcohol-related problems. When people are caught up in a descending spiral of destruction through chemical dependency, we believe it is imperative that they be given every possible chance to break out of that descending pattern and begin the process of productive living. We believe the cost to the individual, the family, industry, and society is increasing. People who are sick with the disease of chemical dependency can be helped. There are methods and ways to help that individual recover a life of health.

The disease of chemical dependency, if left untreated, is 100 percent fatal. Chemical dependency is a spiral downward. It will result in the death of the chemically dependent individual who is unable to implement a recovery plan that includes abstinence. Death arrives from resulting physical deterioration, from accidents, and many times from homicide due to chemically dependent behavior. Therefore, those people suffering from chemical dependency need immediate help. They are experiencing the erosion of their value systems. They are experiencing alienation and isolation from everyone and everything that would provide meaning in their life. It is crucial that these people be given every opportunity for treatment and recovery. Diagnosis will determine the extent of the chemical dependency and the extent of the damage and will aid in determining the kind of treatment and therapy that will be most beneficial to the individual.

II Diagnosis

8 Types of Drinkers

The diagnosis of alcoholism would be an easy task if four conditions were present in our society: (1) All people dependent upon alcohol would be conscious of that fact and would seek guidance and assistance; (2) there would be an adequate number of personnel trained to understand the request of the individual seeking assistance; (3) there would be a reliable and predictably accurate series of diagnostic instruments to indicate the scope and severity of the illness within both the individual and the individual's family; and (4) there would be no negative social repercussions for the individual seeking assistance. If these four conditions were currently operational, diagnosis of alcoholism would not be difficult, and it would not be the complex problem it is today. Inasmuch as ours is not an ideal society, these four factors are not operational.

The diagnosis of alcoholism is an extremely complex and difficult task. What we attempt in this section is to bring order to chaos, to provide a structured way to understand what diagnosis is, and to understand how extremely important it is to treatment.

The purpose of diagnosis is to determine the extent to which an individual is using alcohol as a primary coping device to deal with life, relationships, work, emotions, and reality. Alcoholism is a state into which an individual unwittingly and unconsciously enters, where alcohol has become the primary coping device. If alcohol or other psychotropic drugs are not used as a coping device, if their use is incidental to the individual's life and relation to reality, then the diagnosis of alcoholism may be more difficult. If alcohol or any other psychotropic drug is used as a primary coping mechanism, then the person is diagnosed as chemically dependent.

Let us put this another way. The average individual's life has four general components: family, work, social life, and physical well-being. When the use of alcohol interferes with optimal functioning in any of these areas, when the person is made aware of the interference and continues to persist in the use of chemicals, then that individual is probably chemically dependent. The diagnosis of chemical dependency requires the evidence of dysfunction within an individual's life.

Chemical dependency is not determined because an individual uses alcohol, nor is it confirmed by the quantity consumed. In other words, we are on shaky grounds if we base our diagnosis solely on questions such as how much, when, with whom, and in what situations the individual consumes alcohol. Some people consume large amounts of alcohol, and the consumption does not interfere with their functioning. It is reported that Winston Churchill drank large amounts of brandy all his life, yet he functioned well into advanced age. There are daily drinkers in our culture who do not suffer ill effects from the consumption of alcohol.

The quantity consumed and the frequency of consumption are not in and of themselves indicators of chemical dependency. On the other hand, some people consume relatively small amounts of alcohol on an infrequent basis and become dysfunctional in relation to the alcohol. When this dysfunction occurs, it is one indicator of chemical dependency. Diagnosis, treatment, and assistance is indicated even though dysfunction is the result of relatively small amounts of alcohol consumed infrequently.

As a part of this working definition of alcoholism, it is useful to think of five broad categories or groupings of people who consume alcoholic beverages.

1. *Social drinkers.* These are the individuals whose use is truly minimal to moderate. Alcohol is consumed to enhance or add to the individual's perception of the quality of life. The consumption of alcohol is perceived as part of the "good life;" it is used to enhance meals or is sparingly consumed with friends as an act of sharing. Consumption tends to be a social act, and there are no negative feelings concerning those who choose not to drink.

Many people in this category state that they do not drink alcohol for its mood-altering effect, but it is our opinion that all drinking is for the effect of the alcohol on the central nervous system. Even so, these people drink as a social act, and the use remains constantly minimal to moderate. Alcohol is not consumed to escape reality but rather to enhance a social activity.

2. *Situational drinkers.* These are individuals whose use of alcohol is either absent or minimal to moderate until some significant event in their life places intolerable stress upon them. The use of alcohol will continue so long as the stress remains or until some other coping mechanism becomes apparent to them. The use of alcohol may be highly controlled for periods of time and then may be temporarily out of control.

If the out-of-control situation is long-term, these individuals can move from being situational drinkers into the development of alcoholism. A common illustration of the situational drinker is the person whose spouse has recently died. The survivor, undergoing severe stress and anxiety, begins to consume alcohol. The heavy drinking may subside when the individual recognizes some internal strengths to cope with the situation or when other people provide significant support and stability. If the individual does not discover other coping mechanisms and continues heavy drinking, there is a real risk of developing the disease of alcoholism.

This same kind of dynamic is also seen in people who cannot handle sudden termination of employment. Unemployment may place more stress on them than they can handle. We have often seen such people become situational drinkers.

These people respond dramatically to therapy. They have a history of emotional strength and health. Therapy provides them with the emotional support that enables them to develop coping skills to deal with their traumatic experience. If the trauma can be resolved early enough in therapy, these people may be capable of returning to social drinking, if that was their pattern before the traumatic experience.

3. *Problem drinkers.* These individuals do not appear to be under great stress. There is no major crisis or severe problem creating undue tension. There may well be subtle kinds of problems or pressures, such as the children growing up and leaving home, or the individual's approaching retirement, being passed over at work for a promotion, not succeeding up to expectations, and so on. But none of these events appear overwhelming to the individual.

It may appear that these people are quite capable of handling the tensions existing in their lives, but in reality they are using alcohol as a way to cope with intolerable stress. There will be periods of time when these people consume alcohol to the point of being intoxicated. Sometimes they are involved in a traffic violation and charged with driving while intoxicated (DWI). More frequently, their drinking is work-related, that is, done while entertaining at lunch or after work. It is very common for these people to entertain clients and friends with considerable heavy drinking.

As stress increases the consumption of alcohol increases dramatically and the individuals have no control over their drinking patterns. It is estimated that perhaps 50 percent of all drinkers will experience times of problem drinking. If problem drinkers receive help early in this stage of increased consumption, they will quite frequently reduce the amount of alcohol consumed. In many cases, they become abstinent. The consumption of alcohol assumes less importance.

It is not uncommon for a crisis to occur as a result of a diagnosis of a physical illness. For instance, the individual receives a diagnosis of diabetes. Controlling the diabetes requires a change of lifestyle and of diet. Whereas prior to the physical exam the individual may have been consuming large amounts of alcohol, the diagnosis of diabetes may lead to termination of all alcohol consumption in order to reduce the intake of sugar.

This same dynamic also occurs with some individuals who are picked up by the police and charged with driving while intoxicated. Some people react positively to such an incident and terminate all drinking; this one episode is enough to convince the individual that a change in lifestyle is necessary.

The distinction between problem drinkers and alcoholics is the point of positive response. Problem drinkers will respond positively to advice and help and will often reduce or curtail the consumption of alcohol. Alcoholics will not moderate their consumption in spite of advice or any help offered. Alcoholics are incapable of responding positively to the advice of others.

4. *Severe episodic (binge) drinkers.* These individuals may be minimal to moderate drinkers, or may have been abstinent for a long time, but on more or less regular intervals they will use alcohol in a very out-of-control fashion.

This dynamic is different from that of problem drinkers because severe episodic drinkers are not responding to an identifiable and specific experience or situation that goes beyond coping skills. It is very common for this type of drinker to plan episodes in advance. The planning of episodes can become very sophisticated, involving intricate patterns, such as reserving a hotel room, going out of town, taking a trip for the express purpose of drinking.

The episodic drinking may last only a day, or it may run as long as two weeks of heavy consumption. Frequently the result of binge drinking is hospitalization and detoxification. Binge drinkers are exhibiting alcoholic behavior and must be recognized as alcoholics.

5. *Alcoholic drinkers.* Alcoholic drinkers cannot be identified simply by the quantity of alcohol they consume nor the hour of the day or week when the consumption occurs. All too frequently, people believe alcoholism is a matter of how much is consumed and when. However, alcoholic drinkers may not consume any alcoholic beverage for days, weeks, or months.

A typical behavior pattern is for the alcoholic to "swear off" drinking. This pledge may be sustained for months, but eventually consumption returns. When it does, the alcoholic will be just as intoxicated and just as much an alcoholic as before.

The process of chemical dependency is present in alcoholic drinkers. Drinking occurs because the process of chemical dependency requires the presence of alcohol in the central nervous system. If alcoholic drinkers do not receive help or are not engaged in the recovery process, death is the inevitable result.

There are two identifiable characteristics of every alcoholic drinker. First of all, alcoholic drinkers will have difficulty managing their lives. It may not be apparent at first, but as the drinking continues and as the alcoholism continues to develop, alcoholics will experience a decrease in the ability to function. This dysfunction and unmanageability will eventually affect every area of life. The individual will be in trouble, and the trouble will increase.

The second major identifying factor is that the individual will experience out-of-control drinking. Alcoholic drinkers will be unable to exercise any consistent control over their drinking patterns and the amount consumed. They may be able to exercise control for a period of time but ultimately the out-of-control drinking pattern will manifest itself. Both of these factors feed each other. As the drinking increases and becomes out of control, alcoholic drinkers will experience an increase in unmanageability. This cycle will continue as long as the drinking is present.

These five categories of drinking styles represent the vast majority of our society. The categories are put forward to functionally describe the drinking patterns of our society. On the positive side, the descriptions provide a framework for developing diagnostic methodologies and techniques. Diagnosis must be adaptable to specific individuals. Individuals must receive the proper diagnosis. Obviously, everyone who uses alcohol injudiciously cannot be diagnosed as alcoholic. The personal values and attitudes of the diagnostician cannot be the basis for judgment and decision. Accurate diagnosis is the result of a careful study of drinking patterns and the presence of negative consequences within an individual's life.

There is also a negative side to presenting these five general categories of drinking behavior. It can give the appearance of being easy to categorize an individual's drinking. In fact it is a very difficult task, requiring a great deal of information about a person's life experiences, coping skills, and drinking behavior. People don't fit neatly into categories. Also, chemically dependent people construct denial systems so they will always see themselves as social drinkers, as persons who drink like everyone else. The reader should be cautious and tentative about diagnosing self and others.

According to the National Institute of Alcohol Abuse and Alcoholism, 10 percent of the U.S. population are alcoholic. If you add the number of people who have alcohol-related problems, you come up with a very significant portion of our population. According to a 1977 Gallup Poll, between 1974 and 1976 there was a 50 percent increase in the number of people saying that alcohol was a part of their family problems. The number of people who are either directly or indirectly affected by alcoholic behavior is increasing. For these people, careful diagnosis is the first step toward assistance and help.

There is another compelling reason for diagnosis to be careful and adequate. In our present society, the diagnosis of alcoholism sticks for the rest of an individual's life. Even though these attitudes are changing for the better, our society still deals punitively with the recovering alcoholic. Such an individual may well experience difficulty in obtaining life insurance, medical insurance, employment, admission to a variety of graduate schools, and so on.

Diagnosis of chemical dependency must be conscientiously and judiciously made to protect all parties concerned. If individuals experience penalties for seeking help and assistance, it does not take long for the word to get out to the general public. This punitive behavior is counterproductive for the individual and society. It creates a situation where people who need help, and who might be voluntarily receptive to that help, do not seek help because of the penalties.

9 Signs of Alcoholism

There are many signs and symptoms present in the early to moderate stages of alcoholism. Let's examine a few of them. The following list of symptoms are the ones most often seen in diagnosis. They are listed in order of increasing severity; that is, the symptoms toward the bottom of the list tend to indicate more serious chemical dependency within the individual.

1. *Rationalizing.* According to Webster's *New Collegiate Dictionary,* rationalizing is defined as "attributing one's actions to rational and creditible motives without adequate analysis of true motives." Reasons sound plausible, but they are not true. The individual develops a thinking pattern to find reasons justifying drinking behavior: "Everyone drinks just as much as I do." "I don't drink as much as some of my friends." "I lead a stressful life, therefore I drink to relax." The alcoholic becomes an expert in inventing explanations for drinking behavior and can always invent new alibis if and when they are needed.

2. *Blaming.* The individual blames others for increased drinking and for the resulting behavior: "If my wife were a better wife . . ." "If my old man weren't so mean . . ." "If my husband would only . . ."

3. *Resentment.* The individual hangs on to and nurtures resentnent as an excuse to drink. "I drink because I can't stand [*fill in the blank*]." This may be very obvious to others, but the alcoholic is truly unaware of this behavior, which is operating at an unconscious level within the alcoholic. Nonetheless, the alcoholic will harbor a great deal of

resentment toward self and others and will use this resentment as an excuse for drinking.

4. *Minimizing.* Some individuals consistently minimize the amount and the extent of their consumption. On the surface, this appears as an out-and-out lie. People will tell you they had only two drinks, when in fact they consumed five or six. For some, minimizing occurs because of the guilt they experience as a result of the drinking. For others, minimizing occurs because they simply are not aware of the amount they consume. This is explained in part by the fact that alcohol affects the memory and recall functions of the brain.

5. *Preoccupation.* This symptom takes many forms. The person may be preoccupied with the anticipation of drinking; for instance, the thought of the after work drink begins to occupy the individual's mind more and more each day. Or it may take the form of preoccupation with the act of drinking itself. The individual may spend more and more time at a cocktail lounge, at a drinking partner's home, or in the privacy of home. Preoccupation may take the form of spending more and more time thinking about possible drinking situations: "Let's go out for dinner," "Let's get together after work."

6. *Defense of use.* These individuals tend to defend the right and importance of alcohol consumption. They will construct a more avid defense for drinking than for almost any other behavior. Nonalcoholic people do not construct rationalizations and defenses for drinking alcoholic beverages and spend little time thinking about whether they should have a drink. Alcoholics will construct a defense to prove the rightness and correctness of choosing to consume an alcoholic beverage.

7. *Personality changes.* Some individuals will undergo marked personality changes while under the influence of alcohol. They will become excessively verbal when generally they are very quiet, or they may become extremely depressed instead of happy-go-lucky. They may become abusive to other people when generally they are fairly gentle. The longer the alcoholic drinks, the more pronounced will be the behavioral changes. Eventually, alcohol-induced behavior becomes predominant.

8. *Seeking chemical "highs."* The emotional purpose for drinking is to create a state of tension reduction, a state of euphoria. The alcoholic will drink solely for this purpose. In such instances, there is little socialization while drinking. Reality is too painful when perceived

in a nonchemical mood state. The individual seeks chemical highs and will attempt to recover some previously experienced high.

9. *Urge to use.* Although related to preoccupation, the urge to use has its own distinctive characteristics. Individuals experience periods of an intense urge to drink. For some people, this drive is related to increased moments of stress. The urge will be experienced both physically and emotionally.

10. *Changing tolerance.* Some people will experience a changing tolerance—that is, they must significantly increase their consumption of alcohol to achieve the same results. The converse is also true. Some individuals will get extremely drunk though they have consumed less alcohol. In either event, there is a changing tolerance to alcohol within the central nervous system. Great change in tolerance is a very significant sign.

11. *Attempts to control.* In an attempt to prove to themselves and to others that they are not alcoholic, individuals may construct a very complex control system to reduce or eliminate drinking. Typical examples are to never have more than two drinks; to give up drinking for Lent; to switch to a different type of alcohol, for instance, from Scotch to rum or from beer to wine. Any control system will ultimately result in failure, because the drive for alcohol will destroy the arbitrary controls. Ordinary people don't set controls and limits on their drinking behavior; only those who are attempting to control their drinking problem will construct such systems.

12. *Use at inappropriate times and places.* This behavior runs the gamut from drinking on the job, drinking in the car while driving, having a drink just before a job interview, and so on. Quite simply, normal people with normal drinking habits do not drink on the job, they don't drink while driving down the freeway, and they will not have a drink before a job interview. Such behavior ought to be understood not as deliberate, overt, or conscious. The decision to drink or not to drink is at a much more unconscious level, but at that unconscious level the alcoholic will be motivated to consume alcoholic beverages irrespective of appropriateness.

13. *Changing drinking patterns.* Here drinking incidents occur more frequently, and the amount consumed increases. Drinking may become heavy during free time, or the individual may become drunk more frequently. There is a distinct change in the drinking pattern, which will be observed by those people closest to the alcoholic.

14. *Discomfort with nonusers.* More and more, alcoholics seek the

company of other people who tend to drink as they do. They will become extremely unaccepting of nonusers and dislike socializing where alcohol is not served.

15. *Unpremeditated use.* Individuals will use and abuse alcohol when they had no intentions at all to be drinking. With these episodes, there will be no intent to get drunk; indeed, there may not be any intent to drink at all. But the individuals find themselves in a drinking situation. Such behavior also takes the form of intending to have one or two drinks after work and continuing to drink until the bar closes.

16. *Conflicts of values.* As the drinking progresses into chemical dependency, there will be a very definite shift in values. Although this shift may be subtle, the individual's sense of what is right and wrong will begin to change. The individual's understanding of what constitutes moral and immoral behavior begins to shift. Individuals may at times behave in ways that are in direct conflict with their personal value systems. They then must deal with the guilt produced by actions that are counter to what they believe is right or wrong.

17. *Medicinal use.* No matter what the physical symptoms, alcohol is seen as the accepted medication. As silly as this may sound to the nondrinker and the nonchemically dependent, this is a very common rationalization. Furthermore, the chemically dependent person will appear very sincere and honest as chemical use increases for so called medicinal purposes.

18. *Seeking companion users.* For the chemically dependent, socialization is directly related to chemical use. The individual spends more and more time socializing around consumption of alcohol. In reality, the individual is experiencing the disintegration of intimate relationships and friendships. Time spent with ''drinking buddies'' increases. In reality, the ''drinking buddies'' generally tend not to be the kind of people the alcoholic would have chosen to be with prior to the onset of chemical dependency.

19. *Protecting the supply.* The individual will make sure the supply of alcohol is constantly available, and if necessary will go to great lengths to hide the supply from other people. The supply may be hidden at home, in the garage, at work, in the workshop, and so on. The place is not as important as the fact that the individual is compelled to protect the supply of alcohol.

20. *Verbal or physical abuse.* While under the influence of alcohol, the individual becomes verbally abusive, angry, hostile, and resentful.

In many cases, the verbal abuse is followed with physical abuse and injury.

21. *Arrests related to drinking.* The individual may be arrested for reckless driving or driving while under the influence of alcohol. The individual may be arrested for aggressive destruction of property or physical abuse while under the influence of alcohol.

22. *Blackouts.* The individual will experience amnesia for certain events or periods of time. The time involved may be only a very few minutes or a period of days. For instance, the individual cannot remember what occurred at the party the night before. In severe cases, the amnesia may block out not just hours but a period of days. Individuals experiencing a blackout will be unable to recall what was said, people they were with, things they did, and so forth.

Alcoholism and other forms of chemical dependency are extremely complex diseases, as the human being is an extremely complex system. The presence of any one or two of the symptoms listed above will not automatically constitute a diagnosis of alcoholism. The complex pattern and the combination of these symptoms is important to the diagnostician and will indicate areas of further investigation. Chemically dependent people probably will not be aware of their defense mechanisms. They probably will not be aware of the presence of any of the symptoms. If they are aware of these symptoms, there is a good likelihood that they will minimize the symptoms. Whenever possible, the diagnostician must gather information from other people, preferably members of the family. Assessing all of the available data, the diagnostician will come up with a clinical judgment of diagnosis. The diagnostician must be able to say, "No, this person is not chemically dependent," or "Yes, this person is chemically dependent." If a diagnosis of chemical dependency is affirmed, the diagnostician must be able to determine the extent of damage, which in turn guides recommended treatment procedures.

10 Problems of Diagnosis

For the past several years, there has been a tremendous flood of material presented to the general population regarding chemical dependency. Through newspapers, magazines, radio, and television, the problem of chemical dependency has been widely presented. Why, with all of the information that has been transmitted, is early diagnosis still such a problem for our society?

The answer, although harsh, is quite simple. The very people who should be able to recognize the signs and symptoms of chemical dependency have not been doing their job. There are exceptions in each case, but by and large inadequacy has ruled the day. We have asked patients in our program at St. Mary's to identify by profession the people from whom they sought help for their problems with chemical dependency. We then asked them whether or not they received help and, if so, what kind of assistance they received. Four professional groupings are consistently mentioned: the medical profession, certified psychologists, clergy and religious leaders, and the legal profession. Teachers and school counselors are also mentioned quite frequently if the patient has school-aged children. The response is very consistent and has not significantly varied from the day St. Mary's began its treatment program.

While the dynamics of chemical dependency were increasing, the individual frequently was in contact with the medical profession. There were trips to the physician's office for annual physicals, which turned up nothing that would indicate chemical dependency. Occasionally, the annual physicals would indicate some emotional stress or problem.

Typically, the individual was either given a prescribed medication or referred to a psychologist or psychiatrist. There was little if any conversation regarding lifestyle, drinking patterns, interpersonal relationships, or the individual's means of coping with day-to-day life problems. If there was a physical complaint, the symptoms were observed and directions given to resolve the symptoms.

With some frequency, our patients report that, after repeated trips to a physician's office for a constantly changing list of aches and pains, the physician or nurse began to ask questions about problems at home, at work, and so on. When this occurred, the flood gates opened, and the individual began to pour out the miseries of either being (or living with) a chemically dependent person. For the most part, however, our patients report receiving no sound advice or assistance regarding chemical dependency.

The most common direct assistance offered by a physician was referral to a psychiatrist. All too frequently, family practioners and internists have turned over to psychiatry the problems of chemical dependency. When this has occurred, our patients report that psychiatry treated their alcoholism by prescribing other psychotropic drugs that did not produce any significant therapeutic response to their chemical dependency.

The professional group that has the most immediate and initial contact with chemically dependent people and their families are clergy and religious leaders. Clergy usually have the opportunity to recognize the early to middle stages of alcoholism anywhere from three to five years before the family physician does. The help offered by clergy is often a combination of the following: discussing alcohol as evil and the alcoholic as a sinner; selected readings from scripture; exhortation through prayer; and discussions of free will. Most chemically dependent people who receive help in this form quickly decide that religion has litttle to do with resolving their problems of chemical dependency.

A large number of our patients have worked with psychologists, either in personal counseling or in marriage and family counseling. By and large, the issue of chemical dependency did not surface. The individual and the counselor worked on a lot of other problems, but the central problem of chemical dependency remained hidden.

The legal profession has a great deal of contact with the chemically dependent population, who create a lot of work for attorneys and courts. There are law suits over bad debts, divorces, arrests, appearances in court, and convictions with or without jail sentences. A vast number of people go through the court systems because their behavior is antisocial as a result of chemical use. Unless our legal system recognizes chemical dependency and either provides treatment or refers to treatment, legal problems related to chemical dependency will continue to increase.

It is not surprising that our helping professions have not been more alert and more responsive to the problems of chemical dependency. In the first place, only recently has some education in chemical dependency been incorporated into the professional curriculum. Most professionals have had no training, no education in the dynamics of chemical dependency, and therefore they do not know how to identify potential problems and appropriately respond to them.

Second, each of these professions deals with a very limited aspect of human beings. Each has defined its role to work with a specific part of the human being. When a human condition such as chemical dependency, which cuts across all the parts, exists, then each profession can turn to the next and say that work with chemical dependency belongs someplace else.

There is also a third reason why more responsible work has not been conducted in the past. Chemically dependent people will protect their dependency above all else. While not under the influence of alcohol, alcoholics (at least in the early and middle stages) have the ability to conceal that chemical dependency from almost everyone. If the professional person has not been trained and is not astute in reading signals of chemical dependency, then that professional will probably never recognize it. Chemically dependent people place a higher value on maintaining the dependence than on survival and certainly more than on personal relationships.

Therefore, expecting chemically dependent people to come in and to be open and honest about their dependency is extremely naïve and simplistic. Just as the chemically dependent person constructs an elaborate defense system, so also the family keeps the secret as long as possible. The family is in a desperate struggle, with no place to go. The family members have reasoned, argued, prayed, and manipulated to get the chemically dependent person to straighten out, all to no avail. The stigma of alcoholism is real, and exposure has consequences not only to the alcoholic but to all the members of the family.

Eventually, however, the secret has to break out. The family cannot maintain 100 percent control. The spouse and other family members experience health problems; the whole gamut of physical-emotional symptoms emerge: headaches, gastrointestinal disorders, hypertension, acute anxiety, depression and so on. Alert health-care personnel will recognize that there must be some underlying factors producing the physical-emotional problems.

The following illustrations are typical of confrontations resulting in admission to treatment.

My husband was confronted first by a business partner and two friends who were knowledgeable about chemical dependency. The four of them went over to a counseling center. In the middle of the afternoon he called home and said, "You're not going to be able to guess what happened to me a few minutes ago. I was just confronted with the fact that I have a drinking problem." I think both of us knew. We had talked about our drinking. We knew the kind of messes we got into because of our drinking; that was when our real fighting happened. But we reversed it like most people do — the reason we drank was because of all our problems.

My first reaction was one of real anger, "What do you mean you have a problem?" I was very, very threatened that my drinking partner was leaving. Both of us would keep up with the other. All night long we were very compatible with our drinking. "What are you going to do?" He didn't know, so we talked about it that night. In the back of my mind I knew that something was going to happen to me. The wife of one of the fellows who had been in on my husband's confrontation had been through a treatment center, and I suspected something was going on. Sure as shooting, the next morning at 8:00 she came over. I knew I had reached my doom. She talked to me, and I reacted with the typical fashion of "You don't know me, I'll never drink again," and was very angry and very hostile. Doggone if she didn't come back again that night. My husband had agreed at this point to go through treatment.

He said he was going. That was really threatening to me. I thought I was being closed in on from all sides. I finally agreed to talk with someone at the counseling center the next day. I talked first about my husband's problems and his breakdown. Then the counselor said, "I don't know if you have a problem or not. I'm not going to put you into treatment right now. However, I, don't want you to drink for the next couple of weeks." I knew that I couldn't do that. I got up to leave, came back, and said, "I can't do it." He kind of laughed and said, "I'll get a bed for you too!"

Two of my fraternity brothers still cared enough. Most of the others had given up. One night about two weeks before finals I was really thinking crazy . . . about driving to Illinois to see an uncle who is a counselor. I thought maybe he could fix things for me. I thought I was about to go crazy, about to go looney. Someone called my brother, and he stopped me. I had been drinking all evening. He subdued me and dismantled my car. I ran away and went to a neighborhood bar and drank until my parents found me. They managed to get me back to my brother's apartment. I ran away again, this time to the fraternity house. It was around 4:00 A.M., and by 5:00 A.M. my two friends managed to talk me into entering a treatment program. My initial thought was that people would think I was an alcoholic. And they said, "Damnit, everyone already knows you're an alcoholic, that's not the problem." That really hurt. I thought nobody knew; I thought I was so clever. I even had my checkbook coded so no one could tell how much liquor I had bought. They said, "You're going into treatment." They didn't ask me if I wanted to go, they said, "You're going."

There is a tendency among workers in the field of chemical dependency treatment to be highly critical of the various helping professions (physicians, clergy, attorneys, educators). This negative, critical attitude is nonproductive. Members of these various professions are highly educated people; for the most part, they are trainable and are receptive to education that will increase their capability. Chemical dependency workers cannot sit on the sidelines and remain critical. We must provide the leadership and the training for members of the professions who can be highly competent diagnosticians and very capable of intervening in the process of chemical dependency with their clients.

Just as the medical profession has this opportunity to respond by looking beyond the physical-emotional symptoms, the alert physician, clergy, attorney, or teacher will be presented the symptoms and the signs of emotionally sick families dealing with chemical dependency. As the family controls break down and the secret is out, each profession will see manifestations of the family disorder.

Each has the opportunity to continue to provide professional services while at the same time referring the family to a competent chemical dependency counseling center. This does not mean that all professionals should be competent in the sophisticated techniques of diagnosis. Far from it. They should, however, be aware enough to spot indicators of potential chemical dependency, and they can then follow through by referring for diagnosis and, if warranted, treatment.

Part of the problem of diagnosis is that people tend to view chemical dependency too simplistically. As few as ten years ago, drinking problems (alcoholism) weren't treated as such. The physical complications resulting from alcoholism were treated by the physician, and a psychiatrist treated the behavioral problems. Now the pendulum has swung so that the diagnosis of chemical dependency is seen as the great problem solver. Both approaches are narrow minded.

People who are alcoholics can have just as many psychiatric or mental problems as nonalcoholics. An individual may be disguising other emotional diseases with alcohol. Remove the alcohol, and the other signs and symptoms will become apparent. These have to be recognized and treated. It is the same with physical ailments. In fact, alcoholics tend to have more chronic disease processes going on in them because of their alcoholism. Alcoholics have a higher incidence of diabetes, hypertension, and emphysema than the general population. If the attendant physical illnesses aren't cared for, the alcoholic does not recover from alcoholism, and the other diseases get worse.

Diagnosing alcoholism means also paying serious attention to existing physical illnesses and to existing psychiatric or mental problems. Recovery from alcoholism is not a magical cure for physical ailments or existing psychiatric problems. Care must be provided for the whole person: emotional, social, intellectual, spiritual, and physical. The goal is for the individual to integrate these five areas into one. As the individual begins to integrate a personality that incorporates these five areas, then the true health of that individual becomes a possibility. One stumbling block, therefore, is that a narrow and limited view of diagnosis will result in fragmented efforts at treatment.

A second stumbling block is that sometimes you discover you are treating the wrong family member or that you should be working with multiple patients from the same family. Alcoholics tend to come from sick families. Sick families tend to produce alcoholics. Alcoholics tend to make families sick. The disease process is contagious. Other members of the family may not be using chemicals, but they may be just as emotionally sick. When involved with diagnosis, you have to be ready to diagnose and work with several family members. An individual living in a sick family tends to be as sick as the family; the individual member tends to take on the characteristics of the family. Human beings are interrelated with others in their environment. A family is more than the sum total of the individual members; the family also develops a life of its own that has power and influence over the individual members. Diagnosis must take this dynamic into account.

We must understand that the focus of diagnosis is to determine whether or not the individual needs treatment. Diagnosis may also indicate that other people surrounding the chemically dependent person may need treatment.

Another erroneous belief is that the alcoholic is a morally corrupt person, a sinner of the first rank. There is no doubt that many alcoholics believe this. It has been the message delivered to them from the first time they experienced intoxication. They have heard the exhortation, "Change your ways, leave Godlessness behind, and walk the paths of righteousness." They have said it to themselves, they have heard it from their family, their friends, and their clergy. To attack a chemically dependent person by saying, "You are a morally corrupt person," provides a destructive label for that individual.

All these dynamics are present during the diagnosis. It is the task of the diagnostician to:

- confirm the presence or absence of chemical dependency.
- assess the extent and scope if chemical dependency is present.
- assess existing strengths within the individual
- develop appropriate recommendations for treatment.

Many people come through St. Mary's Hospital for diagnosis. When the diagnosis confirms the existence of chemical dependency, some of those people leave, refusing treatment. Most remain. Of those who remain, 70-80 percent develop an integrated lifestyle during treatment sufficient for them to arrest the process of chemical dependency.

11 The Importance of Intervention

Where there is strong suspicion that an individual or family are struggling with chemical dependency, a tremendous effort is required to attempt diagnosis and treatment. The diagnostician should not expect to receive information spontaneously to corroborate a diagnosis of chemical dependency. The necessary information and data to form a comprehensive picture of the chemical use pattern will have to be obtained from several sources. The most efficient way to receive this data is to have the people around the individual develop carefully constructed sequential behavior descriptions over a period of time. This data is then presented to the individual in a nonthreatening manner, allowing the individual to express self-perceptions regarding the chemical use pattern. The rules for this process, which is called *Intervention,* were first described by Vernon E. Johnson in *I'll Quit Tomorrow:*

1. Meaningful persons must present the facts or data. That is they must be people who do exert real influence upon the sick person. His forms of denial can and will sweep aside the efforts of others. The meaningful persons may be members of the family . . . although such members will almost always need help in gaining sufficient emotional stabilization to carry out the task. The intervenors may be professionals, such as physicians or clergy, if they personally possess information which is useful. This would include descriptions of physical complications or behavioral patterns indicating the presence of the disease.

The most effective intervenors, however, because they are the most meaningful of all, are employers or the members of management at the level next above the chemical dependent person. Individuals tend to put their own greatest value as people on their productivity, so the boss is the most meaningful person.

In any case, for the most part, intervention should not be attempted alone, although it can be done. Groups of at least two or three seem most effective. They tend to support each other in getting the task accomplished successfully, and also have the necessary weight to break through to reality.

2. The data presented should be specific and descriptive of events which have happened or conditions which exist. "I was there when you insulted our client, and it was obvious to both the client and to me that you'd had too many," or "The word around the office is not to send clients to you after lunch. The others often feel you aren't in shape to take care of them." Obviously evidence is strongest when it is first hand.

Opinions are to be avoided, along with all generalizations. "I think you have been drinking too much," or "I think you ought to quit drinking entirely," are worse than useless. All such general opinions do is raise the defenses still higher and make the approach to reality more difficult.

3. The tone of the confrontation should not be judgmental. The data should show concern; in truth, the facts are simply items to demonstrate the legitimacy of the concern being expressed. "I am really worried about what has been happening to you, and these are the facts available to me which will give you the reasons why I am so concerned." The list of facts follows.

4. The chief evidence should be tied directly into drinking whenever possible. "After the company picnic last Saturday, I saw you leave a bit under the weather. I assumed that your wife would do the driving, but I learned that you drove nearly 100 mph on the freeway with your family in the car." The more general data should only be used to support the examples of drinking. "Your production has gone down this year."

5. The evidence of behavior should be presented in some detail, to give the sick person a panoramic view of himself during a given period of time. He himself does not and cannot have this view because of his deluded condition. He is out of touch with reality. His greatest need is to be confronted by it. Sound movies or tapes of some of his drinking episodes will do it best. No argument is possible,

no denial can be made. There it is on the silver screen or on tape, acting and sounding like that. ("My God, I didn't know I had hurt so many people so much!") The intervenors are to act for the silver screen. "This is reality!" "Reality is not what you have been believing it was!"

6. The goal of the intervention, through the presentation of this material, is to have him see and accept enough reality so that however grudgingly, he can accept in turn his need for help.

7. At this point, the available choices acceptable to the intervenors may be offered. And in many sections of the country there are choices. The key person confronting the alcoholic may say, "Since abstinence is a basic requirement, there are alternatives before us: this treatment center, that hospital, or AA. Which help will you use?" Allowing them, in some way, to be a part of the decision making is to offer him some sense of dignity, which is obviously important. Firmness here, however, is again necessary. His defenses can and very likely will regroup quickly unless he is sure the intervenors mean what they say (pp. 49-51).

Vernon Johnson has aptly described a very exciting and effective process for getting a person into treatment. We employ his principles of intervention in our program. We see the effectiveness of presenting alternate views of reality to the chemically dependent person. There is no doubt in our minds that this intervention process is a responsible, caring act, and it works. Our experience at St. Mary's indicates that, in order to carry out the intervention process in a responsible fashion, we should recognize a few cautions. These are:

1. The people accumulating the data may not be honest or objective in their data. If they have suffered, they may, in fact, be vindictive.

2. The people accumulating the data may have already decided that the individual is chemically dependent and report only data to support that conclusion.

3. The subject of the intervention may be so overwhelmed by the people present that he or she will agree to anything.

4. The subject of the intervention may have enough significant medical or psychological problems as to be unable to rationally respond to confrontation.

5. Many individuals conducting intervention are insufficiently trained to recognize the danger signs of this process.

6. Intervention should be conducted only by trained qualified people.

The goal of this intervention process, the hopeful result, is that the individual will agree to a diagnosis determining whether or not chemical dependency exists; and, if it does, to participate in the treatment process.

III Treatment

12 Background of Treatment

The purpose of this section is to remove popular mistaken images about therapy and treatment. Treatment is not magic; it does not need to be discussed in hushed tones. Treatment is the process that enables the individual to live a productive life without the use of mood-altering chemicals.

St. Mary's Rehabilitation Centers offers five programs for adult chemical dependency treatment:

- In-Patient
- Out-Patient
- Family Therapy
- Aftercare
- Talbot Hall

Each of these programs maintains its own staff for administration, supervision, and therapy. All the programs share common resources whenever possible. All share a common philosophical approach to chemical dependency treatment and hold the same goals and expected outcomes of treatment. Before we examine these goals and expected outcomes, it is useful to examine some of the assumptions and the philosophy that underlie all the programs, for it is the common philosophy and the common set of assumptions that result in a unified and cohesive program of treatment.

A discussion of treatment must address the problems associated with the process of recovery. Given the developmental stages of alcoholism, it is little wonder that attention must be focused on the necessity to constantly reinforce learning accomplished during treatment. During the process of becoming chemically dependent, the individual experienced deep emotional learning that affected his or her ability to cope with reality.

Regardless of the fact that this deep emotional learning was ultimately destructive, it was nonetheless that individual's way of coping with a disintegrating world. For many individuals, this process covered a span of years. New learning acquired during a few short weeks of intensive treatment is only a beginning. The individual must experience constant reinforcement over a protracted period of time if a developing new lifestyle is to be realized.

During treatment, the chemically dependent person begins the development of new coping skills to deal it with reality in a drug-free manner. The disease of alcoholism has stripped away strong effective coping skills. Developing coping skills is a long-term process. To move from a position of inadequate coping skills to a position of coping skills adequate to deal with reality is a painful process that requires the development of personal adequacy (a quality not present when the person enters treatment).

Every person who leaves the treatment center is going to face a painful and not-too-gentle world. Some people will not acquire sufficient strength during treatment to endure the world outside. When their limits of endurance are reached, they may return to drinking. Hopefully, a return into treatment will be seen as a step in the right direction and not be perceived as absolute failure.

Another factor contributing to problems in the process of recovery is the fact that the individual returns to a living and working context that may not be changed. Although tremendous effort is made during treatment to work with family members and significant friends, they can be just as resistant to change as is the chemically dependent person. Other people in the home and work context may be just as sick as the person in treatment. If they cannot experience healing, if they are unable to begin development of a new lifestyle, then people returning from treatment are reentering a sick world. The majority of people reentering this kind of world will slip into the familiar old patterns of destructive behavior.

An associated problem of reentry is that the individual returns to home, work, and friends where the use of chemicals has been and continues to be a way of life. To live in that context, to live and work with people who do use alcohol may be asking too much of an individual who has only recently begun to understand that he or she can live without alcohol. A life possible without the consumption of alcohol may be only dimly understood. Perhaps the individual has a sense that such a lifestyle can be accomplished but has not experienced this new lifestyle with enough strength to carry through situations where other people are drinking and where the consumption of alcohol is the expected rule.

The development of an alcohol-free lifestyle is a tremendous alteration in the individual's life. The individual has begun the process of probing, poking around, and examining bits and pieces of life long ago forgotten. If a person has spent years relating to self, others, and work in a medicated state, then time is required to gain a sense of comfort in an alcohol-free life. The individual experiences deep emotional pain and stress. The individual is constantly asking the question, "Is all this pain really worth it?" The healing process is slow, and during the course of time the individual is experiencing stress, frustration, and pain.

The chemically dependent person has generally been lacking in intimate relationships. Certainly there have been no drug-free intimate relationships. To learn how to be intimate, to learn how to receive as well as to give intimacy is a whole new task for the individual. The strength, support, and stability that result from intimate relationships are forces to maintain sobriety, yet intimate relationships take time to develop. The most to be expected during treatment is that the individual will begin to experience the development of intimacy. The individual is moving from a world of isolation and loneliness to a world of relationships.

During treatment, the individual is learning to cope with life in a nonchemical way. During treatment, and certainly after treatment, the individual must find ways to cope with anxiety, boredom, depression, anger, and the like. The individual must face situations and events that produce these kinds of emotional responses. Learning to cope without the use of alcohol will in itself produce anxiety and depression. The chemically dependent person is attempting to behave in ways foreign to his or her previous lifestyle.

The chemically dependent person has been accustomed to medicating all experiences of discomfort; now that individual must learn to cope in nonmedicated ways. The individual needs to experience relationships with other chemically dependent people who are maintaining a lifestyle of sobriety. The individual needs to experience at least one other person (and hopefully many) who can present a successful model of how to live without alcohol. This matter of role modeling is extremely important to the recovery process. The individual needs ongoing situations where he or she can talk honestly and search for ways to strengthen self and resolve problems. The individual needs to discover new ways of socializing nonchemically. Treatment is structured to allow the patient maximum possibility of meeting these needs. The time and the experiences after treatment cannot be so clearly structured.

AA has accomplished more than any other organization in enabling people to maintain sobriety. One of the reasons for AA's effectiveness is that it does provide the immediate structure for support, for socializing, and for successful role modeling. For this reason, St. Mary's requires weekly AA attendance for all participants in the Treatment and Aftercare Programs. Participation in AA provides immediate contact with people who have developed ways to maintain life styles of sobriety, ways to cope with the stress and anxiety resulting from chemical dependency.

Let us turn in the next several chapters to a description of the five treatment programs. To aid this narrative, four former patients at St. Mary's have related their experiences to illustrate the treatment methodologies. Using fictitious names, the four are:

Phyllis: married with children. Both she and her husband participated in treatment.

Paul: married with children, an engineer.

Charlie: a college student in his early twenties.

Ann: not an alcoholic. She participated with her alcoholic husband.

13 The In-Patient Program

The In-Patient Program is a four- to five-week stay in the hospital. Patients are admitted into the program by their own physicians. Patients are provided semiprivate rooms; family and friends may visit at regularly scheduled visiting hours daily and on weekends.

The intake interview determines the social history of the patient: employment, marital status, family history, education, military service, chemical use, prior participation in treatment, religious affiliation, leisure activities, and medical or psychological problems. If possible, other family members will be interviewed for a more comprehensive report of patients' drinking histories. (See Appendix for examples of admission interview forms.)

Individuals who are intoxicated at the time of admission are placed in the detoxification program. Patients may be in this program for three or four days, depending upon the amount of time required for thorough detoxification. This step is necessary to allow the body time to detoxify the chemicals so the patient can enter the treatment program in a sober condition. There is no reason to begin any therapy if the patient is intoxicated. Life support systems are available if needed. Medication is available to reduce the physical symptoms of detoxification and to reduce any dangerous effects, for example, anticonvulsive medication.

The admitting physician will complete the physical examination and all laboratory and X-ray testing as part of the admitting examination. This thorough physical examination is conducted to provide the basis for diagnosis of any coexisting disease entities present within the patient, for instance, hypertension, heart disease, diabetes, emphysema, arthritis, malignancies, arteriosclerosis, skin disease, allergies, bronchiectasis, and so on. At this time, initial efforts are made to uncover existing psychiatric or psychological problems. If any disease entities are diagnosed, therapy will begin immediately for treatment, control, and regulation of these diseases. This treatment occurs simultaneously with alcoholism treatment. Consultants in various medical specialties are available upon request of the admitting physician.

As the symptomatology of detoxification subsides and patients become functional, they enter the orientation process. Through lecture and discussion, patients receive information about chemical dependency and how the process of chemical dependency affects them, and some knowledge of their expected participation in the treatment process. Patients receive basic information on the function of the treatment center. They are oriented to the expectations of the staff, the ways in which family members will participate, and the expectations for their personal behavior. They receive information concerning the basic therapy group and lecture methodologies used in the program. Information is presented to begin the process of assisting patients to understand personal defense mechanisms and to identify feelings and emotional states.

When orientation is concluded, patients are assigned counselors and therapy groups. The patients will work with these therapy groups throughout their stay in the program. Working with each group is a therapeutic team composed of the counselor, assigned nursing staff, and a physician. All of these people are integral to the therapeutic process. The team meets periodically to assess patients' status, to gain further knowledge of the group's functioning, and to determine if there are additional ways in which any staff member can work to enhance the patients' progress.

The therapy group meets regularly five days a week. This group is composed of ten patients and the previously described team members. The group becomes that "place" where individual behavior is analyzed. Defense systems are examined. Patients will experience learning and growth in the ability to identify and respond to emotional states. They have the opportunity to identify needed coping skills and to work for their development. Confrontation, caring, and development of intimate friendships are the dynamics present in the therapy group.

Three times a day there are lectures covering a wide range of subjects related to the five dimensions of the human being: emotional, societal, intellectual, spiritual, and physical.[1] Among the lectures are:

- Introduction to the Philosophy and Lifestyle of AA
- Individual lectures on the Twelve Steps of AA
- Potential Anatomical Effects of Alcohol
- The Alcoholic and the Family
- Family Therapy
- The Dynamics of Recovery
- Sexuality
- The Dynamics of Forgiveness
- The Delusional Memory System
- Alcoholism Treatment
- Group Dynamics
- Reflection on Recovery
- Common Sense Philosophy
- Progression of Addiction
- Alcoholism, a Treatable Disease
- Other Chemical Addictions
- The Disease of Alcoholism
- Values

During the course of the program, patients will also participate in individual counseling with their assigned counselors as well as with other staff as the need arises.

Every effort is given to provide individual counseling, family counseling, lectures to increase intellectual awareness, time for socialization, time for work on spiritual growth, and time with family members.

Phyllis: *When I came in I was totally smashed. They medicated me with either Valium or Librium. For two days I was really spacey and zonked out and I don't remember much. I do remember getting very angry at the counselor who conducted Orientation. Then I cooled from that and went into my therapy group. For the first four or five days I really didn't do much other than sit and halfway listen. I had a lot of psychiatric problems prior to treatment . . . shock treatments and three or four hospitalizations for breakdowns, depression. I attempted two suicides and had been hospitalized. The first week at St. Mary's I was thinking, ''I don't belong here.'' I was still not willing*

---

[1]See Appendix for a typical daily schedule.

to see it as a chemical dependency problem. I was really thoroughly convinced I was insane, and my behavior was pretty doggone insane. "I don't belong here — I belong over in the psych ward." It took quite a while for it to sink in that I really wasn't insane.

The therapy group is so all-important. For someone who is not in touch with their feelings, who really doesn't know what's going on with their emotions, it is a learning process to actually feel feelings. To say, "I'm angry about something," and have someone come back to you, "You don't really sound angry — what else might be going on?" — that sort of a process. You might be really hurting and not even know it. All of a sudden you start talking, the tears start coming, and you really get in touch with that hurt. You label it, and you know what's going on.

The second week of treatment I remember getting in touch with my anger. It was a horrible experience. My husband's group was meeting in the lounge right outside my group. I went storming out of the room and walked right through my husband's group. As I walked down the hall I heard everyone laughing, saying "There goes his wife." After really being angry and hostile I went back to my group and discovered that I hadn't been rejected. As a matter of fact, it was good that I had been real. I really did a turn around from that point on and thought, "My God, I finally am somebody and I can let go of all this garbage inside of me — I'm still okay. I don't have to be phoney any longer." It was just like a bolt of lightning! From that point my treatment progressed very well. It's hard to put into words. I never had much feedback from anyone, at least negative feedback, in my entire life. I protected myself, I'm sure. Because my self-worth was so low, heaven forbid that anyone should criticize me. So, in therapy group the patient interaction was the first time anyone gave me feedback . . . some pretty honest feedback. This was the first time anyone had ever really been straight with me. It gave me permission to start opening up.

For me it was being able to get rid of some of the phoney facade. I was the kind of person that was always immaculately dressed, always had makeup on even when I came out of the bathroom to go to breakfast. God forbid that anyone would see me other than that. My whole self-worth was low. In any event, I was sure crappy inside. I'll never forget when I came into treatment, I had two garment bags of clothes and suitcases. As I progressed, I kept sending the clothes home with our sitter and just wore blue jeans. That was a real turn-around for me . . . to be able to get up, run a comb through my hair, scrub my face, maybe put on some lipstick, and go down to breakfast. It was just the neatest thing to hear people say "Hey, it's really nice to see you just be yourself—without all that facade." It was good to receive feedback from people: what they were hearing, and "What do you mean by that?" or "Gee, that sounds kind of phoney, what's all that about?"—that sort of thing. A lot of good things happened sitting at a meal table or playing cards. We would play cards at night, or someone would bring a guitar, and we'd sit around and sing; we'd pop popcorn . . . all these added so much. I learned to take risks in a protective environment. Mingling with the patients, the patient interaction, taking some risks and being accepted were some of the greater parts of the treatment.

I remember the staff saying, "Recovery is a long, slow process." It wasn't until I lived through that long, slow process that I realized how terribly important and how true that is. It is a long process of learning.

Charlie: I didn't know anything about St. Mary's at the time. First, I had to learn I had a disease, rather than considering myself an immoral and crazy person. This was really hard for me. I guess it's hard for most people. I had a strong religious background and I figured God would never look at me for what I'd done. Second, I had to get in touch with my feelings. Maybe this doesn't sound fantastic— people think of treatment as something spectacular—feelings, that doesn't sound like treatment! But when you have been medicating for a number of years and trying not to feel, then getting in touch with feelings is a really difficult thing.

When I say get in touch with feelings, I mean to recognize feelings. When you've got that knot in the pit of your stomach, when you are really scared, then talk about it. So you're scared . . . there's nothing wrong with being scared. It's not a crime against society or against your manhood. When you hurt, then say it. Be honest with how you are feeling and talk about those feelings. Be honest with yourself.

When I first came in, they would ask me some questions about my behavior, and ask me how I felt. I was miffed at first. That was the extent of my feeling anger at that time. I wouldn't admit to being angry. Eventually I learned I was minimizing what I really felt.

It's like having your behavior on a slide, and the group puts the slide under a microscope and they let you see close up. The analogy often used is that of a mirror. The group points out your behavior and reflects it so you can take a look at it. Very often I did not like what I saw. I didn't want to admit to a lot of my behavior.

I learned that I was basically a very insecure person. I had to have a lot of support all the time to be calm. I also learned I had a tendency to be grandiose and that I was a perfectionist. I learned a lot about myself. I learned a lot of good things about me too. I recognized a lot of good feelings, a lot of happy feelings. The first time I began to feel good I told my therapy group, "I feel strange"—it was almost that I was telling them that I should be feeling worse. They just started to laugh, and I couldn't understand until they explained to me that I was just feeling good. I had started to feel happy.

Near the conclusion of therapy, patients prepare for leaving. In AA terminology, patients participate in the Fourth Step and Fifth Step work. The Fourth Step requires patients to construct autobiographical statements that detail personal strengths and weaknesses and identify the alcoholic behaviors to be eliminated. These are statements providing an assessment of the patient's life up to and including participation in treatment. The Fifth Step requires patients to share the autobiographical material with at least one other person. Through this step, patients bring their emotional and intellectual states into unity. What patients feel and desire are synchronized with their value systems. Through the process of analysis and "making public" their lives, patients have the opportunity to experience forgiveness and release from the past.

During the final week of treatment, patients and counselors will develop a discharge plan. This written plan specifies the steps and actions the patients will take to maintain a lifestyle of sobriety after leaving the treatment center. Included in this plan will be participation

Figure 8

in AA and the Aftercare Program. The plan also includes additional steps to be taken to strengthen interpersonal relationships and family life. This plan takes into account living arrangements, work setting, and use of leisure time.

A ceremony is conducted on the patients' final day of participation in the treatment program. With all patients and staff participating, the departing patients will publicly present the behaviors that resulted in their entering the treatment program, their assessment of participation in the treatment program, and their plans for maintaining a lifestyle of sobriety. Patients are presented a medallion like that in Figure 8 and graduated from the treatment program.

14 The Out-Patient Program

The Out-Patient Program is similar to the In-Patient, with its content organized into five nights a week for four weeks. Patients are admitted by their physicians. There is a preadmission interview, and patients are accepted into the Out-Patient Program if the interviewer believes they are capable of maintaining a lifestyle required for admission. This lifestyle requires (1) the maintenance of sobriety (abstinence from the mood altering substances), (2) the ability to continue employment without disruption, and (3) the ability to sustain home life and personal life. If these conditions are met, patients will be admitted to the Out-Patient rather than the In-Patient program.

The spouse or significant other is expected to attend as a participant in the program. We use the term *significant other,* a term that may not be meaningful to many people. What we discovered is that work with a patient is only a part of the necessary step toward recovery. We need also to provide treatment within the context of the patient's personal relationships. In many cases, this means we work with the husband or wife. But for many of our patients there is not a spouse to participate in the treatment program. We strongly urge these people to enlist the assistance of someone with whom they feel close, someone with whom they have a significant relationship.

Monday through Thursday evenings the schedule is divided into therapy groups of ten patients plus a counselor; significant others are also divided into therapy groups with a counselor. The last part of the evening the patients and significant others are together in a couples' therapy group. In this way, attention can be given to the special needs of patients and significant others, each in their own groups. Having the couple together for the last part of the evening provides the opportunity to examine the couple's relationship and to assist in the recovery and development of healthy relationships for each couple.

Ann: *The first hour we attended lectures about the disease of alcoholism. After that, my husband and I attended separate therapy groups. The last part of the evening we attended a couples' therapy group. Usually we sat across from each other rather than together. The group and the leaders talked about what it means to live with an alcoholic, and we examined our marriage behavior. We received a lot of support and a lot of feedback; the group was interested in feelings. They want to know how you are feeling, how you are trying to handle it, and how you react.*

I was always a very controlled person, and I had always pushed down my anger. When I left the group session the first night, I didn't like the counselor very much. I thought she was unkind, she hurt people with her talking. By the time I left St. Mary's, after those five grueling weeks, I felt she really cared.

We took a look at our powerlessness over alcoholism and how our lives had become unmanageable. We discussed our situations, what we had experienced. Previously I never thought about feelings. It never occurred to me that I had anything but positive feelings. I knew that sometimes I was happy, but I never thought about any other feelings. I didn't think about being afraid or scared or angry. Now I know when I am afraid, angry, or scared, and I also know it is all right to experience these feelings.

The program helped me from the standpoint of finding out that I wasn't very unique. There were all of these people who had experienced the same things that I had experienced, and I had never shared with anyone what had gone on in my life — the depression, the sadness, all of the confusion. It was helpful to know there were other people with similar problems, that they were willing to talk about them.

Friday evenings are modified slightly to accommodate the inclusion of children. There are lectures for everyone; counseling groups for patients, spouses or significant others, and children; and family therapy, treating the family as a unit.

Paul: *I ended up at St. Mary's through the grace of God. I was aware I had a drinking problem, but I didn't consider myself an alcoholic. I didn't drink daily. I was a Friday night drinker, a weekend type. Once in a while I would go out to lunch and drink more than I should. Two things scared me about my drinking. I had gone back to work on several occasions having drunk too much. I probably went undetected by my superiors, but I was scared to death that I was going to slip and be detected. I had a lot of fear about that. Also, my relationship with my wife had deteriorated very, very badly.*

Before treatment the only person who told me I might be an alcoholic was my wife. No one else had ever directly confronted me and said, "Have you considered the possibility that you might be an alcoholic?" Being as defensive as I was while drinking, it's possible that someone might have, but I don't have any recollection of someone confronting me.

I had an incident the last time I went out and got drunk. I went out with a few of the guys from work, celebrating some excuse, intending to have a couple of beers. I called my wife and said that I was going to be home at 6:30. I fully intended to. I had absolutely no desire to go out and get drunk. I ended up getting very, very drunk that evening. I woke up from a blackout. Blackouts had become very frequent for me. I was blacking out more easily than I had in the past. I was convinced that I wasn't an alcoholic because I didn't drink regularly. I didn't drink in the morning. I had a lot of other reasons why I believed I wasn't an alcoholic. Anyway, that evening I apparently blacked out in the bar. The next awareness I had, I was beating my wife. It scared the living daylights out of me. I had in the past slapped my wife; I felt that any woman who would say the things that she said deserved to be slapped. I would rationalize this to myself, even though I hated myself for doing it, even though I didn't think that it was something appropriate. Anyway, my wife was really scared. Fortunately, she had the courage to call the police. They gave me the option of going to the Detox Center. I said, "No way. I didn't need the Detox Center." They tried to encourage me to go, and I refused. They said that the alternative would be to book me. Finally my wife agreed to sign an assault charge. So they hauled me down to the jail. Going to jail was quite an experience for me, having never been near one before. I thought at this point, "I'm emotionally sick. Anybody who would beat their wife and do a lot of the other things I do is a sick person." Finally I decided that I would contact the chemical

*dependency staff at work. I wanted help. I was scared to death of
what was happening. I hated myself for what I had done, and I
wanted help.*

*I finally got in touch with one of the staff at work. The counselor's
immediate response was, "You need to be in a treatment center. I
think St. Mary's Hospital is the best treatment center and program. If
you want me to, I can arrange an interview for you immediately."*

*I hated myself very much for the things I had done while drinking.
I'm not necessarily tying it all to drinking. I just hated myself very
much. I was relieved to be going to St. Mary's. I did want some help
very, very badly. I was also scared to death of what I was getting
myself into. I don't think I really expected to go in and quit drinking. I
went in that first day a little bit hopeful that maybe I could get some
help, but extremely afraid that I might have to talk about who I am, or
what was going on with me, and I did not want to talk about my
behavior.*

*I went into treatment under a lot of pressure. I was concerned
about being arrested for the assault. About a week later I was in court
and pleaded guilty to assault and received a year's probation — under
the condition that I go to AA for a year. When I went into treatment, I
went with the attitude that I had a drinking problem and I needed
some help to control it. I really didn't understand where I was, or
what I was getting into; I had no concept that I was an alcoholic, just
that I wanted some help. I didn't like what was going on with me. I
didn't think that I needed the chemical dependency help as much as
psychiatric help.*

*I had never been in a group therapy situation in my life prior to St.
Mary's. The first night was scary for me. I had no idea what I was
getting into. I had a woman counselor who I thought was a power-
hungry bitch who liked to control men. After going through treatment, I think she is one of the most beautiful women I have ever met
in my life. I do remember that first evening getting very angry at her,
thinking that she was a bitch the way she would confront people and
tell them what she thought of them. I don't think that she confronted
me that evening. She was nice to me that first evening, but I was
scared to death of her. I didn't like her, and I thought that she was not
a nice woman at all. She wasn't my image of what a nice woman
should be.*

*Once I completed my First Step, which took a lot of pain and guts
and sweat to do, it was like I had found the path. I had finally made a*

First Step. The patient group after that was far less difficult, and I wasn't so extremely fearful. We talked about how I felt — trying to get to the point where I could recognize the feelings with myself and express those feelings. It was the counselor who would precipitate my participation. She would make me angry or sad or whatever, attempting to get an emotional reaction in order to help. The group would give feedback to the individual, to help this individual know that he or she was conning or whatever.

It was exhausting, but I recognized something good happening to me. Although it was physically exhausting, it was something that I looked forward to very much. We had lectures on the physical disease in terms of what's going on with your body and how it affects you, lectures on the feelings aspects of the disease, and the problems of dealing with the disease. I recall a lot of lectures that I could relate to very easily, which made me feel comfortable because I felt people were talking about what was affecting me. We had a series of lectures, also, to differentiate between alcoholism as immoral behavior and alcoholism as a disease. My behavior was the result of a sickness. An alcoholic with this disease is similar to an epileptic or someone who has behavior anomalies. It is essential for an alcoholic to understand this part of the disease and not to believe that ''I am a bad person.''

I had four weeks of treatment, going on a daily basis to the treatment center — five nights a week, Monday through Friday. We arrived at 5:00 P.M., and typically it would get over at 9:15 P.M., sometimes a little later. It was tough. My wife was also involved in the Out-Patient Program. She met me there every evening, and we spent 4-4½ hours a night there. It was very exhausting. We would end up coming home at the end of a session and talk until 1:00 or 2:00 A.M.

Five o'clock was the starting time and we were expected to be there very promptly. Our counselor would let us know if we were not holding up to what was expected. At 5:00 we received an hour lecture. Then we would have a short break and go into a therapy group with other patients. This would last an hour and a half to two hours. So between 7:40 and 8:00 P.M. we would break, and then we would go into a couples' group with my counselor. That group would last until 9:00-9:30 P.M. In the couples' group session we would concentrate on the relationships and communications with couples and other problems that were being experienced.

My wife and I sat in the middle; the rest of the group sat around us.

My wife talked about my behavior during my years of drinking, the feelings that she had, the hurt, the things I had done to damage our relationship. That was helpful to me in doing my First Step. It helped me understand how she felt about my drinking. Some of the things I wasn't very consciously aware of, so it was helpful for me to be confronted by my wife in the group. It was extremely helpful, because I don't think either of us were comfortable in talking about my drinking behavior. This was a first step in becoming comfortable as we talked about our pain.

My wife knew what was going on with me, and I could also see what was going on with her. I didn't appreciate the problems or the symptoms she experienced with the alcoholism. I had drunk heavily from the first day we married. Our whole marriage relationship (thirteen years of marriage) involved drinking. I didn't have any appreciation whatsoever for the problems of my wife. The couples' group helped me to appreciate what my wife had been through. It made my recovery easier, and it definitely helped us get a start on our relationship.

The thing that I found most helpful was talking with my wife in the group. I couldn't possibly have done that without the group. I didn't have the courage to do it without someone pushing me into it. The counselor would get us into a situation where we would volunteer something that was very much troubling one of us. We would then talk about what was going on with us. In particular, it is helpful to have the group point out things that we were totally unaware of. We were playing games with one another, not being fully honest with one another, not leveling with each other, and trying to control one another. I became aware of things I was doing, particularly with my wife. I wasn't honestly communicating with her, and I wasn't letting her know how I felt.

I could relate to the problems and experiences other couples experienced. This made me more aware of who I really am. There was so much similarity with others in the group. I saw other people who were just as afraid as I to express their feelings. It gave us support. We discovered we were not unique, and that made it easier for us to start working. I was particularly appreciative of my wife's involvement in therapy. It wasn't me doing something for myself and then coming back to my home and trying to work alone. For many years I had been drinking, and our relationship was terrible. Her participation made my recovery a whole lot easier. I feel strongly that

*the family involvement, and particularly the spouse involvement, is
extremely beneficial.*

In preparation for leaving the treatment program, patients follow
the same procedures as outlined in the In-Patient Program. Patients
are required to conduct a Fourth Step and a Fifth Step. After this work
is completed, there is a "graduation" program each Friday night for
those departing.

15 The Family Therapy Program

Chemical dependency is a family illness. The disease not only directly affects its victim, it also takes its toll on family members and significant others in the addicted person's life. The family suffers frequently from diminished communication, deteriorating relationships, disabling preoccupation with the disease, and an increasing presence of emotional pain.

Treatment directed exclusively at the identified patient produces little real impact upon the family that has become ill. The family receiving no therapy concurrent with the patient remains essentially unchanged. The unhealthy family environment stifles the personal growth and development of its members and jeopardizes the recovery of the patient. Thus the legitimate goals of chemical dependency therapy must include service for both patients and their families.

At the time of admission to the In-Patient or Out-Patient Treatment Program, the patient and his or her family or significant other are informed of the Family Therapy Program, and their involvement is encouraged. Involvement usually occurs in the third week of treatment. Objectives in the development of a Family Program are to:

1. respond more fully and effectively to the health-care needs of the chemically dependent family.

2. enhance the patient treatment experience by adding more meaningful depth to the therapy provided.

3. improve the prognosis by making primary relationships between patients and significant others better.

4. move toward prevention of further chemical dependency in families of addicted individuals (children of alcoholics have an alarmingly high statistical chance of becoming addicted themselves).

Pertinent, specific information about chemical dependency as a family illness is provided. The program guides participants through a careful examination of the effects of chemical dependency upon individual family members as well as upon the family as a unit. We identify the various family problems that arise with addiction and facilitate the development of personal and interpersonal skills to deal creatively with the problems. Recovery plans are developed and implemented, including referrals to the Aftercare Program. The Family Program offers a comprehensive approach to the family illness. Program components include:

- A specialized family orientation.
- A significant other specific lecture series.
- Daily significant others group therapy.
- Continuous and concentrated daily family groups.
- Individual family conferences.
- Extensive reading.
- Final evaluation and referral.

The Family Program is designed to respond to the current therapy needs of the patients and families in both our In-Patient and Out-Patient Programs. Therapy is directed at individuals within the family as well as at the family as a whole. It is our belief that such a program improves the treatment experience, enhances the family unit, improves patient prognosis, and provides meaningful preventive measures for family members.

Phyllis: *As far as treatment is concerned, family involvement is terribly important. Putting people into treatment and then back into a sick environment is either impossible or a painfully slow process. The things that the spouse gets into, the rationalizations, the guilt that they feel, the blaming, it's just horrendous. I really think that sometimes the spouse is more sick than the patient. She or he doesn't even have the booze to blame it on. It's a tough society that still reinforces the feelings such as "If I had been a better wife or if I had been a better husband. . . ."*

Ann: *The program helped me understand how the disease of alcoholism touches the entire family. I was exhibiting bizarre behavior as the spouse of an alcoholic. That was a real eyeopener. There was a lot of feedback; people could see things in me that I couldn't see myself.*

For the first time, relationships were being established, because previously I had superficial ways of relating to my husband and other people. I never rocked the boat. I wouldn't make waves for anything. Now we are communicating . . . we clear the air, we discuss feelings . . . and we are going someplace with our relationship.

I felt there was something wrong with me, that things were not good, but I minimized them. I had a lot of distorted vision and distorted feelings, because I wanted things to be good. I felt there was something wrong with me, that my husband didn't really love me. I looked at other people and thought, "Gee, they are happily married, I wonder what they do right and what I am doing wrong?" I felt that something in myself was causing the poor relationships and the unhappy marriage. I felt that it must be something that I say or do or the way I act. I must drive him to drink. And then I found out that there were other people who loved their husbands, alcoholic husbands, and that alcohol caused the behavior problems. This really helped.

We expect spouses or primary significant others to spend the family week in residence; such involvement would include room, board, and therapy. Children participate, generally on a nonresident, out-patient basis. An evaluation at the end of the week results in an extension of Family Program involvements or a referral to Aftercare status.

16 The Aftercare Program

The Aftercare Program is conducted for all patients who have participated in the In-Patient, the Out-Patient, and the Family Therapy Programs. Aftercare is a two-year therapy program. Patients and spouses or significant others are expected to attend this program two evenings per week for two years.

Recognizing that chemical dependency is a chronic disease requiring extensive support for patients and their families after treatment, St. Mary's provides such support at levels and in ways that will increase the gains made in the treatment process. We believe the two years following In-Patient treatment are the most crucial in terms of recovery for both patients and their families. Therefore, we provide opportunity for the maintenance of sobriety and for improvement in the quality of life.

St. Mary's provides two years of Aftercare to patients and their families by involving them in weekly activities to maintain their contact with this treatment center and give them needed support during this period when crucial readjustments of all kinds are generally being made.

Paul: *I started to be afraid of leaving early in the last week. I started thinking about not coming to the hospital afterward, even though it was pretty physically exhausting and emotionally exhausting. I was scared, and I can remember strong feelings of real fear — not having that place to go back to after work. I was very much afraid of*

"Where am I going to go from here?" People had talked about the Aftercare Program, but I didn't know what it was all about. I didn't have any confidence that the Aftercare Program was going to give me what I needed to maintain my sobriety and continue what I had started.

I had begun feeling good, being able to talk about what was going on with me and feeling the relief, the letting go of a whole lot of things that I had been hiding. I was feeling better about myself. I was able to talk about myself and who I really was. I was afraid of going away from that place and not being able to continue this. I just didn't know what to expect. When they talked about AA, I thought, "What the hell are they doing that for? I'm not interested in AA; that's a bunch of old fallen down drunks on skid row." I had the impression that AA was that kind of organization—I didn't understand it. One of my biggest fears in considering treatment was that my friends were drinking buddies, and I was scared to death about what I would do when I chose not to drink. What do I do for friends? I didn't know what real friends could be. I now have warmer friendships with more people in AA and growth groups than I have ever experienced in my life.

I find that somebody who slips back into drinking hasn't been going regularly to AA. I was scared not to go. I was deathly afraid not to go to my growth group, because I didn't want to go back to drinking. I got into an AA club, and still am. I wouldn't miss it. I'll give up almost everything for AA. I started off thinking that my AA squad was a bunch of stiff people who didn't share very much. I have come to know that they are some of the most beautiful people in my life. I care very much for and love the people in my growth group. It is something that has been—and is—one of the most important things in my life.

Before treatment I presented myself as a very self-reliant, independent person who didn't need other people. I think now I make people aware of the fact that I do need people. I like to let people know that I do need people. I am no longer afraid to need other people. I used to consider it weak to need other people. I don't consider it weak any longer.

Every Friday evening there was a family session. We were encouraged to bring our children. We had a ten-year-old daughter and a twelve-year-old son. They participated in some of the family evenings and had good reactions to it. My children did get involved in the family group in the treatment. I feel strongly that this was a significant thing. Seeing some of the movies and hearing lectures gave us a jumping-off point, a vehicle, from which to begin talking. It is okay to talk about what happened. The kids had been scared to death to say anything to me about my drinking. For years I had been telling them it was not okay to talk about my drinking and their feelings. These things were standing in the way of our relationship. Now it is okay for them to talk to me about how they feel. Family therapy gave us a starting point to talk as a family about what was going on. So I feel very, very strongly about that aspect of the treatment that involved all of my family, my children included. It made it easier for me to start my recovery, being able to work with them and getting them involved. They are involved in the Aftercare Program. They go to the PreAlateen Program.* One of the things I discovered is that I like my children so much more than I ever did before. I realize the change is in me — it isn't that my kids have changed. That's so rewarding and satisfying to me; it gives me motivation and incentive to work harder.

Ann: It was a scary feeling to leave the treatment program because I felt, "If it's taken me all these years to get this sick, it must take a long time to get well." It was really scary knowing that I had so much work to do . . . fortunately there was the Aftercare Program . . . it gave me the support and the assistance I needed to reestablish my health, and it gave me the courage to reestablish a marriage relationship.

Charlie: The Aftercare Program requires you to attend at least one AA meeting a week and participate in a weekly growth group for two years, an extension of treatment. It continues the process begun in treatment. For me, the group was not as confrontive, but it did provide accurate feedback. The term tough love is something you can value. A lot of times they told me things I didn't want to hear . . . they told me the truth. There is a lot of care. I think if a stranger walked into the room he or she would think, "What a rotten bunch of people! How can they talk to each other that way?" What that person wouldn't realize is that these people care about each

---

* The Pre-Alateen Program is for family members six to twelve years old. The Alateen Program is for family members thirteen to eighteen years old. Both programs meet weekly and work with participants to further knowledge about chemical dependency, build self-esteem, develop interpersonal relationships, and prevent chemical dependency among members.

other. You learn to trust each other, and therefore you speak honestly and truthfully.

Phyllis: *I had two mixed, very distinct feelings about leaving St. Mary's. First, I was scared to death, scared to leave this protective environment. Second, I was totally elated, a little cocky and a little arrogant. I was very thankful that I was going to be coming back to St. Mary's on a daily basis for the family therapy, that was real security to me.*

The six days between meetings of the Aftercare group probably were just as valuable as the group itself. We would get feedback in group and then think about it, put it on and wear it for a few days. We probably would have given individual counseling or couple counseling a try, but we had been through that before, too. It was important to have other people who had been through the pain to be able to say, "I really know what you're talking about — we were there." "Here are some things we tried." Our kids were involved too. They started working on their feelings and working to eliminate any guilt that they might have experienced. They had thought they were responsible for our alcoholism.

One of the key elements is the Pre-Alateen Program. Now it is really okay for my kids to say, "Mother, I'm really angry with you." I don't respond and say "Don't talk to your mother that way!" It is great for us to be able to express what we are feeling.

Before, I was a person with no self-worth. I always had material and tangible things. But that's really shaky. My whole self-image was on how I looked and how I presented myself to other people . . . and all of a sudden I no longer looked like the centerfold in Playboy Magazine. *That's pretty shaky. But that was my mindset. Now I say, "Hey, you are a person; you go through a normal aging process like everyone else." I also learned to take risks. They didn't wipe me out as a person. I succeed at some things. I make mistakes at some things. I get a second chance at some things. But it's just okay to be who I am.*

In the Aftercare Program, we have four primary methods of support:

1. Individual counseling services.
2. Growth Groups.
3. Heavy involvement with Alcoholics Anonymous, Alanon, and Alateen groups.

4. Special groups and counseling in addition to or in place of the previous methods of support, to fit individual needs.

The Aftercare Program is based on the following beliefs:

• Patients continue to have problems that they prefer to discuss with a counselor rather than in a group situation.

• Patients and their families need peer groups in which they can evaluate their own progress; learn how to accept and give help; share experiences faced outside of treatment; help them feel less unique; help them form desirable friendships; improve their communication skills within the family and outside of it; receive encouragement and rewards for continued sobriety and improvement; and receive practice and encouragement in taking risks and in building a history of success and developing strength to accept personal responsibility. Patients and spouses usually need to improve communications in their marriage relationship.

• Patients and their families need to start a lifestyle that they can depend upon for support after they have completed the two-year Aftercare Program. For this reason, we believe in thorough indoctrination and practice in living according to the tenets of Alcoholics Anonymous, Alanon, and Alateen. We believe that regular, fully participating attendance in Alcoholics Anonymous offers the patient the best ongoing means presently available for maintaining sobriety. We believe the Alanon offers a permanent lifestyle that is very beneficial to patients' significant others. We believe that participation in Alateen helps patients' children to understand and resolve the immediate problems with chemical dependency in the family. It also provides these young people with worthwhile standards that will sustain them throughout life.

17 The Talbot Hall Halfway House

Talbot Hall, St. Mary's halfway house, is an important part of the continuum of care for those chemically dependent patients who need a protective environment to make major life adjustments during the first months following in-patient treatment. Talbot Hall helps to fill a great need in the Minneapolis-St. Paul area for those patients whose lives have been most seriously disrupted by the illness of chemical dependency, and whose resocialization would be extremely dubious without the aftercare of such a facility. The residents are former patients of St. Mary's Alcoholic Treatment Unit, and referrals are made by counselors of the Alcoholic Treatment Unit.

Residents are carefully screened so that only those applicants who will derive the maximum benefit from a halfway house environment are admitted. Each resident selects goals, and achievement toward these goals is periodically reviewed with the Resident Coordinator. Attendance at two house meetings per week is required, in addition to the two weekly meetings of the Aftercare Program. Residents must also adhere to house rules, including a curfew.

Charlie: *Seven months after treatment I was accepted into Talbot Hall. They wouldn't accept me at first — only after I convinced them I intended to maintain sobriety. My initial thought was that it was a place to throw my bags. As time progressed, I realized it was a place where I could be honest, where people would accept me for who I* *was. It was an atmosphere where I could grow, learn to be myself, and get to know others. It's not just a place to sleep. They care about you. You're like a family. There are group meetings, and all the residents are required to attend. There was a lot of learning how to do things together instead of in isolation. Talbot Hall became my temporary home. Most of the people living there had daytime jobs, but those of us who didn't would spend a lot of time helping each other. The staff was always available and would spend time with us. Living with other people who had similar experiences was a real support for me. There was a fairly constant turnover of people, so we had to face the leaving of a good friend and learn to meet new people.*

I was talking with my father recently about treatment and the changes that have taken place in my life. He said, "You know, at first I thought you were too young to be an alcoholic. I could never see a twenty-one year old college student being an alcoholic." That was part of my delusion too. That was a really good excuse for my not admitting my alcoholism.

I'm glad I joined the human race. The way I joined was by admitting that I make mistakes and yet realizing the world doesn't stop; it's okay to feel hurt, to feel angry, to feel good. I'm more realistic about what I can do and what I can't do.

The purposes of Talbot Hall are many. The adjustment of a chemically dependent person to a new way of life is overwhelming and often impossible; when a patient returns to a peer group or family setting where other members are using chemicals, the patient will experience a very difficult time establishing a lifestyle of abstinence.

As a general rule the person leaving treatment is still very unstable in many aspects of life. The individual has entered treatment from an environment that has endorsed and supported the abuse of chemicals. Some come from family settings that have been destructive to all family members. Some have been isolated from their families, their only contact being with peer groups that have also been destructive to interpersonal relationships. Others come from employment situations that have been equally destructive to the individuals.

The first change the person experiences at Talbot Hall is being in constant contact with chemically free people. This contact accomplishes many things for the chemically dependent person. It demonstrates that abstinence is possible, that it is possible to function without the use of chemicals. It provides an opportunity for the person to make new friends who are also abstinent, friends who are excited about developing interpersonal relationships in a chemically-free environment. These new friends can discuss their problems, regardless of the severity. This contact allows the residents to learn more about themselves, their feelings, their past way of life and behavior, and their abuse of chemicals.

Residents of Talbot Hall become a family in which members can express themselves freely to one another. Care and concern for other residents develops as each individual grows and matures. Many residents experience the development of family ties with other residents, ties stronger and more meaningful than those experienced in their pre-treatment home life.

A charting system is used to continually update and evaluate progress of all residents. Each resident must develop goals and objectives to be achieved during residency. Progress and change, or the lack of progress and change, are recorded as part of the permanent record of each resident. This record contains the treatment history, physical and psychological testing data, and activities undertaken while in Talbot Hall. This record provides the information needed by the staff to counsel and guide each resident.

The Talbot Hall Program is designed to permit the resident full opportunity to achieve personal goals and objectives. Restrictions are minimal, but they must be obeyed. Time away from Talbot Hall must be accounted for; residents must sign in and out. Curfew is midnight. Each resident is expected to work either as a paid employee or as a volunteer, must remain chemically free at all times, and must participate in regularly scheduled group meetings as well as individual counseling.

Prospective residents are interviewed by current residents. After acceptance into Talbot Hall, any resident who does not conform to the rules or who does not enter into the family style of living is asked to leave at a meeting of the whole group.

18 Issues of Treatment

All of the treatment programs at St. Mary's are based on a holistic understanding of the human being. For purposes of examining treatment content and in order to develop in integrated therapy approach, we perceive the human being as a composite of five clusters or groupings of needs: emotional, societal, intellectual, spiritual, and physical. Individual needs cannot be neatly compartmentalized and segregated into one of the five areas; each cluster of needs is interrelated with the other four (see Figure 1, p. xvi).

This image of clusters permits us to develop a comprehensive treatment program designed to treat the whole person. Our program content and our staff represent an interdisciplinary approach. In this way, we are able to ensure care for the total person. Decisions for program content, for filling staff vacancies, and for encouraging innovation in individual and group therapy approaches are made from a holistic point of view.

This image of clusters enables us to pinpoint the areas in the patient's life where attention must be given. In what areas of the patient's life is the process of chemical dependency exhibited? All five areas may not be equally disrupted. All areas must be examined and diagnostic and treatment plans designed for each individual. Without this image of clusters, accuracy is more difficult; pain and dysfunction appear to be amorphous, appear to be enveloping all of the patient's behavior. With the image of clusters, we can diagnose and specify treatment more appropriate to the individual patient.

Within the world of chemical dependency treatment, there are divergent views concerning the use of medication during treatment. One position is that the goal of treatment is absolutely medication-free living, that work with the patient is not only to eliminate alcohol but to terminate all use of any psychotropic drugs. This position is advanced by many members of AA. These people place a great deal of pressure on patients to give up medication, to make a unilateral decision to stop taking all medication, even physician-prescribed medicines. There is a danger in this action. If the patient is manic depressive or schizophrenic, for example, the termination of prescribed medication can exacerbate the psychotic state, which increases the chances that the patient will resume drinking.

Our goal is not an absolute medication-free existence. Medication may be necessary for treatment or control of major psychiatric or physical problems. Where medication is necessary, it will be prescribed. For instance, Antabuse, a chemical that blocks the normal metabolism of alcohol and results in the build-up of a. specific substance within the blood (acetaldehyde), will be prescribed for those patients requiring such medication. People taking Antabuse will become severely ill if they consume alcohol. Patients using Antabuse will quickly learn not to drink any alcohol; that is, if they don't believe the doctor in the first place. At St. Mary's, we do not withhold medication that will enhance treatment and recovery.

This philosophical argument arises from the fact that many chemically dependent people have been heavily medicated as a way to control alcoholism. In many cases, the reliance on medication to control alcoholism resulted in further deterioration of the patient's health. This phenomenon is present enough that it has produced an overreaction in the therapy world, and for many the gospel has become "chemically free."

Some treatment centers will not prescribe medication. It is our view that this philosophy has produced problems, because patients have been denied medications needed for other disease states. There is no need for medication to treat alcoholism; but associated diseases may require medication. Our approach is to treat the whole person. To arbitrarily deny the possibility of medication is to deny care to the total person.

Patients have stayed away from treatment centers (or they have not been initially referred) because of the mistaken assumption that all treatment must be chemically free. This simply is not so, but the philosophical argument continues within the world of chemical dependency treatment.

We believe there is a spiritual side to the human being. One of the important clusters or groupings of needs centers around a spiritual understanding of the universe. In the world of chemical dependency treatment, this is a commonly accepted view of the universe and provides a great deal of strength and support to the restructuring and refashioning of lifestyles for chemically dependent people. One of the key components in treatment is development of an understanding of spirituality. This is a difficult and sometimes tedious task requiring time and effort. It is a task only initiated during treatment. After treatment, the individual must continue to develop understanding concerning the spiritual nature of the universe.

The issue of spirituality arises because of a dominant characteristic of our society. One of the strong forces mitigating against recovery is the societal attitude that spirituality is not a significant contribution to understanding reality. "Sophisticated adults don't believe in a spiritual reality." Sophisticated adults may in fact debate and argue philosophical approaches to the understanding of life, but this is far from deepening an individual's understanding of spirituality.

When chemically dependent people leave St. Mary's treatment center, they leave on a spiritual quest. However, they have come to understand that they cannot deny the spiritual side of their nature. They understand that, if they continue to deny this part of their nature, they will not be dealing with reality as a whole person.

When they return to their families, when they return to their homes and work, hopefully they have the wisdom and the strength to continue the deepening and sophistication of their spiritual understanding in spite of guranteed skepticism on the outside. We continue our efforts to aid individuals in understanding themselves in relationship to reality, which includes spirituality.

In order to assist the development of spirituality, we have as an integral part of our staff individuals who are designated as pastoral care counselors, and who have specific backgrounds and training in the field of spirituality.

We believe people recovering from the disease of chemical dependency must develop and restore a sense of balance to their lives — balance in playing, loving, working, eating, sleeping, and so on. These people need to learn how to regain a sense of balance in their relationships. They need to learn what a normal day and week look like. Integral to a balanced life is paying attention to spiritual reality.

19 Goals of Treatment

Viewing the individual as a whole by examining the cluster of five basic human needs, we are constantly developing reasonable expectations of therapeutic outcomes. What are reasonable goals for therapy? Because the dynamics of chemical dependency are so complex within the human being, it is too simplistic to say that the goal of therapy is "to teach Uncle Charlie not to drink." Because alcoholism is not an immoral condition, we will not construct goals of therapy to teach people how to be moral. Because through chemical dependency the individual loses control of self, we do not construct goals that depend upon sheer personal willpower for success.

We do believe it is possible for individuals to grow. We believe it is possible for individuals to respond to love, direction, and caring confrontations. We believe life is a continuing process. Reality can and does shift and change for people. Development and growth are possible. On the basis of these beliefs, we have developed outcomes of therapy that are possible to achieve and that enhance the individual's life, aiding in development and growth and the restoration of direction and accomplishment.

Following is a partial list of practical and achievable therapeutic outcomes. The chemically dependent individual will:

• *develop a lifestyle of sobriety.* The process of chemical dependency is reversible. It can be arrested, and the individual can recover from the downward spiral of its effects. To assure continued recovery, sobriety is a must. Treatment begins the first steps of sobriety, but the individual must develop a lifestyle in which sobriety is ever present.

• *experience a reasonable, mature attitude toward prescriptive medication.* The individual will develop the mindset and the ability to differentiate between his or her experience of chemical dependency and the occasional necessity for use of prescriptive medicines. The individual will develop an open-minded attitude rather than arbitrarily condemning all prescriptive medications.

• *adopt the philosophy and lifestyle of Alcoholics Anonymous.* Regular, continued participation in AA is emphasized and should be accompanied by accepting and living the philosophy of AA.

• *understand the process of chemical dependency.* Our treatment programs provide a sound intellectual base for rationally understanding what occurs within the individual suffering the disease of chemical dependency. The individual will understand the serious and detrimental effects of chemical dependency upon the five clusters or groupings of human needs.

• *understand the dynamics of addiction.* The individual will have increased knowledge of psychotropic drugs and their effects on the mind, body, and personality.

• *gain knowledge of how mood-altering chemicals have affected "my" life.* Through the lectures and individual and group counseling, the individual will gain new knowledge and insight into how his or her life has been negatively affected, behavior has been out of control, and personal relationships have been destroyed.

• *understand how to develop a chemically free lifestyle.* The individual will have begun to develop an integrated lifestyle, knowing that it is achievable, and experiencing some of the ways to attain the goal.

• *develop a greater degree of self-knowledge.* Through therapy, the individual will have gained insights into his or her self, will have a clearer picture of personal strengths and weaknesses, and will have discovered self as authentic and real.

• *understand defensive attitudes.* Through self-examination and individual and group counseling, the individual will understand types of defensive behavior and will be able to identify how defensive behaviors are used.

• *experience a reduction of defensive attitudes.* The individual will rationally and emotionally understand the misuses of defensive behavior and will identify defensive behaviors he or she uses.

• *develop some degree of self-acceptance.* One of the major negative consequences of chemical dependency is destruction of the ability for self-acceptance. Chemically dependent behavior is destructive of all positive self-images. The individual will experience the beginnings of self-acceptance.

• *experience the growth of ego strength.* The individual will begin to develop inner strength based on a sense of self-worth, and will experience success in understanding personal strengths.

• *develop the ability to talk about the self openly.* Most people suffering the disease of chemical dependency are not able to openly express feelings and moods. With the growth of self-acceptance and ego strength will come the ability to risk sharing with others what has long remained hidden and buried.

• *experience a reduction of the sense of uniqueness.* Through the development of relationships and through group therapy, the individual will emotionally understand that he or she is not unique, that others have experienced similar thoughts and behaviors. The sense of isolation and "aloneness" will begin to diminish.

• *begin to understand what is meant by love of self, others, and God.* As the sense of uniqueness diminishes, as the sense of self-worth increases, the individual will begin to experience just how interrelated he or she is to all of life.

• *experience a sense of comfort in dealing with reality.* The chemically dependent person lives with ever increasing amounts of pain and anxiety. As the disease intensifies, so does the pain and anxiety. Initially, the use of mood-altering drugs will mask the pain and will dull the perception of anxiety. But it is the nature of the disease to eventually produce even more pain and more anxiety. Through treatment, the individual will experience a reduction of anxiety and pain associated with living more fully in reality.

• *understand the necessity of living one day at a time.* Recovery is a long-term struggle. Viewed from the beginning, it looks impossible to many people. To manage recovery, to manage creative living, the individual must develop the ability to break time into manageable segments. "Don't try to do the whole thing in one day." The patient will experience the personal strength that comes with being able to work on the task of living by taking it one step at a time. This not only suggests a sequence of activities (such as the Twelve Steps of AA), it also means developing an attitude toward life that you will live in the here and now and not be overwhelmed by worrying about weeks, months, or years from now.

• *understand the need to relinquish control and manipulation.*

Control and manipulation are highly refined coping skills for most chemically dependent people. The patient will understand that other coping mechanisms are more appropriate and certainly more effective for producing stability and meaningful relationships.

• *understand what is meant by peace and serenity.* For many people, the giving up of control and manipulation will result in an increase of serenity. The individual will understand how a sense of personal peace and serenity is developed.

• *develop acceptance of the fact that "my life has been out of control."* The chemically dependent person experiences a decrease in the control of his or her life. It is essential to recognize that the psychotropic drugs were a major factor in this loss of self-control. It is only through development of sobriety that a sense of self-determination can be reestablished.

• *experience reduction of loneliness and alienation.* Through treatment, the patient will begin to develop relationships (or reestablish relationships) that result in support and the sense of "being with others."

• *develop a sense of being responsible.* The individual will come to the realization that he or she is ultimately responsible for feelings and behaviors. There is no one else nor any other circumstance to blame. Personal responsibility will be developing.

• *experience reduction in the amount of resentment and hostility.* Many chemically dependent people carry great amounts of hostility and resentment toward self, others, and life in general. During treatment, the patient will begin to experience reduction of resentment and hostility and will no longer need to express resentment and hostility inappropriately.

• *experience reduction in the amount of anxiety.* In concert with the reduction in control and manipulation, the patient will become less anxious. With the increasing sense of peace and serenity, the patient will become more "now" oriented and more realistic about skills and abilities to cope.

• *experience reduction in the amount of guilt and shame.* Past behavior provides the chemically dependent person with all the raw material needed to experience shame and guilt. Through treatment, the patient will experience forgiveness and will understand the destructive effects of guilt and shame.

• *develop the ability to relate and identify with others.* As the sense of uniqueness and isolation are diminishing, the individual will experi ence an increasing ability to develop relationships with others and will discover how to identify with and relate to other people.

• *experience the recognition of interdependence.* Isolation, control, manipulation, and uniqueness prohibit an understanding of interdependence. As these negative characteristics diminish, the individual will begin to experience the support and strength of interdependence.

• *understand what chemicals have been used for in life.* The patient will gain an understanding of how chemicals have been used to modify and medicate the perception of reality. He or she will begin to understand that use of mood-altering chemicals was a destructive way to cope with reality.

• *understand healthy coping mechanisms available.* Through lecture and counseling, the patient will begin to perceive coping strengths heretofore hidden. The patient will discover productive coping mechanisms never developed to the level of effectiveness.

• *understand that the use of chemicals is destroying his or her life.* The patient will gain the knowledge of how the use of mood-altering chemicals is destructive and will eventually affect (if not already) life physically, intellectually, emotionally, socially, and spiritually.

• *develop the ability to tolerate the pain of reality.* Through development of relationships, through the increase in ego strength and self-acceptance, the individual will discover an ability to withstand a harsh reality that previously would have been catastrophic. Vulnerability will diminish; the ability to cope with pain will increase.

• *experience decrease of stress.* Through increased coping ability, the patient will experience a decrease in stress. As new ways of viewing reality are incorporated within personal attitudes and values, the experienced degree of stress will diminish.

• *gain awareness of individual potential.* Chemical dependency results in the loss of positive self-image and the reduction of social, mental and physical skills. With sobriety, the patient will regain lost abilities as well as a sense of worth and potential.

• *develop the ability to live in the reality of here and now.* The patient will experience a reduction of being driven by the past, and anxieties for the future will diminish. The patient will begin the development of living in the present, dealing with what has to be undertaken now, and experiencing fully the reality of the moment.

• *develop tools to cope with existential reality.* The individual will develop ways to cope with life when reality appears shaky and there is no perceived ground for stability. These coping skills will be developed in the context of personal relationships and reinforcement of personal strengths.

• *increase understanding of what is meant by sexuality.* The process of chemical dependency negatively affects human sexuality in terms of deteriorating physical performance, values, and interpersonal relationships. The patient will begin to understand himself or herself as a sexual human being within the context of sobriety. This means values are examined, and many times new values have to be constructed.

• *develop new acquaintances and friends.* Most patients enter treatment with limited friendships, as chemical dependency has eroded the ability to sustain friendships. Many patients must experience new friendships that are not based on the taking of mood-altering chemicals. Drinking buddies no longer exist. New friends, new acquaintances must be discovered.

• *develop knowledge regarding the complexity of others.* Just as the patient discovers how complex a human being he or she is, so also must the patient discover the same about others. With diminishing uniqueness, the patient will discover intricacies within others that he or she could not see with the use of mood-altering chemicals.

• *develop a sense of acceptance of others.* The patient needs to experience an acceptance of other people. New values, new ways of behaving, differing outlooks on life will need to be accepted if friendships and acquaintances are to be developed.

• *begin to understand how everyone needs relationships with others.* Other people will begin to increase in importance. The patient will experience how important other people are for care, support, love, and confrontation. The patient will discover other people as a source of strength for coping with anxiety, stress, and so on.

• *strengthen the family bonds.* Many patients are alienated from other family members. Behavior and attitude shifts as the result of chemical dependency have created chasms between spouses, parents, brothers, and sisters. The patient will discover ways to attempt reconciliation and ways to strengthen what is usually a very fragile and disruptive family life.

• *improve marital relationships.* If the patient is married, it is safe to assume that the marriage relations are strained at best, and usually close to the breaking point. Through treatment, both husband and wife will receive assistance in understanding ways to improve communications and to strengthen the marriage relationship.

• *develop a basic concept of the knowledge of God–Higher Power.*

The process of chemical dependency has effectively diminished or destroyed any positive concepts of God. Through lecture, counseling, and personal contact with other patients, the patient will begin the process of rediscovering old and gaining new concepts of God that are positive and constructive, values that provide strength and support.

This is by no means a complete list of expected therapeutic outcomes, but it is enough to provide an introduction to the way St. Mary's approaches treatment.

Treatment is very complex, because people are very complex and because chemical dependency is a very complex process. But even though treatment is complex, it doesn't require magic, and it ought not to be surrounded with erroneous images and stereotypes. St. Mary's treatment programs work with a cross-section of the American population. Most patients are ordinary people, very few come off skid row. Our treatment programs are designed to provide therapy for people suffering the disease of chemical dependency — this means husbands and wives, mothers and fathers, brothers and sisters, from every kind of neighborhood, every economic background and every age.

Therapy exists to assist chemically dependent people as they develop a lifestyle of sobriety and to provide the setting where they can discover strength in themselves, in others, and in God — strengths that will improve the quality of personal lives.

Through the support of St. Mary's, the efforts of the program staff, and the five treatment programs, thousands of people are now maintaining sobriety. Their spouses, families, and significant others are experiencing a quality of life they once thought impossible.

We must continue to create a receptive attitude toward treatment in our society. This is crucial because there is the greatest chance for therapeutic success in the early stages, when the individual is experiencing minimal or moderate problems. Previously, we referred to the process of chemical dependency as a descending spiral. The higher on that spiral the individual is upon entering treatment, the less emotional, psychological, intellectual, social, and spiritual damage there will be. This is a universal principle of therapy, regardless of the disease — it is true also for hypertension, diabetes, emphysema, and so on.

Therefore, one of the greatest challenges is early diagnosis and treatment tailored to the current life needs of the individual. Unfortunately, diagnosis is easiest when the individual is in the later stages of alcoholism; that is, when behavior is directly related to alcohol consumption, when the individual cannot cope with alcohol, and when there is physical damage, for example, to the nervous system, the pancreas, or the liver. In these cases, diagnosis is quite clear. However, it is also true that expectations for treatment and therapy are reduced the further down the spiral the individual goes.

In the later states of alcoholism, therapy results are not very good, for either the short term or the long term. Because early intervention and early treatment enhance the individual's chances for recovery, it is important to understand how to identify the presence of a developing chemical dependency upon alcohol.

The charts in Figures 9–11 describe the effects of drinking, the probable results if drinking is not terminated, and the prognosis for treatment and recovery.

Early Stage

	Effects	Prognosis If Treated	Probable results If Untreated
Emotional	Irritability, depression, anxiety, guilt, shame	Reversal to positive mental attitude	Increasing emotional dysfunction
Social	Marriage dysfunction Disintegration of relationships	Integrated relationships	Divorce, separation, alienation
Intellectual	Minimal memory defects Minimal decrease in cognitive ability	Total recovery	Increasing evidence of organic brain damage
Spiritual	Beginning disintegration of value system	Return to former values	Total disintegration of value system
Physical	Change in blood chemistry observable only in lab studies	Easily reversed	Early liver damage

Figure 9

Middle Stage

	Effects	Prognosis If Treated	Probable Results If Untreated
Emotional	Severe depression High anxiety Deep shame, guilt, anger, resentment, hostility	Total reversal and return to positive emotional state	Psychiatric disintegration Suicide
Social	Marital breakdown Loss of all relationships, loneliness, alienation	Return to integrated relationships	Divorce Alienation Suicide
Intellectual	Increasing cognative disability. Memory loss Blackouts	Significant improvement	Organic brain damage
Spiritual	Loss of value system Loss of concept of God Desolation	Return to value system Serenity Spiritual fulfillment	Suicide
Physical	Fatty infiltration of liver Alcoholic hepatitis Nerve damage Alcoholic gastritis	Total reversal of damage	Cirrhosis of liver Chronic pancreatitis Gastrointestinal bleeding Heart damage

Figure 10

Late Stage

	Effects	Prognosis If Treated	Probable Results If Untreated
Emotional	Despair	Significant improvement	Suicide
	Depression		
	Apathy		
Social	Desocialization	Moderate improvement	Continued disintegration
	Depersonalization		
Intellectual	Confusion	Moderate improvement	Custodial care
	Disorientation		
	Irrationality		
Spiritual	Total loss of value system	Moderate improvement	Continued disintegration
	Alienation from God		Suicide
	Loss of concept of spirituality		
Physical	Cirrhosis	Minimal improvement	Death
	Chronic pancreatitis		
	Heart damage		
	Hypertension		

Figure 11

IV Prevention

20 Treatment Is Not Enough

On the basis of our experience at St. Mary's, we know it is possible to provide effective, competent treatment for people suffering the disease of chemical dependency. We know how to implement a very effective treatment program. The steps and procedures that will lead to the establishment of treatment centers are well documented.

The number of health-care organizations competently treating chemical dependency is growing throughout the nation. The administration and management of treatment, staff selection and training, program development, and treatment methods are well enough established for other health-care systems to initiate their own efforts in the treatment of chemical dependency. Competent care and treatment exist; there is no need to reinvent the wheel. We are working within the health-care profession to establish additional treatment centers throughout the nation.

One of the difficulties is that treatment centers tend to be clustered in a few sections of our country. Many of our major metropolitan areas have no centers designed specifically for the treatment of chemical dependency. If treatment exists at all in these cities, it will be found either as an acute medical care unit that offers detoxification services or as a part of the psychiatric unit of a public or private hospital.

Most communities do provide detoxification, but detoxification is not treatment. Once the person is detoxified and released, he or she returns to the drinking environment. We believe treatment designed specifically for chemical dependency should be available throughout this country. Inasmuch as chemical dependency exists within the general population in every region, in every age group, in large or small communities, several treatment centers should be available in each region of this country.

The metropolitan area of Minneapolis-St. Paul is one of the few where a cluster of treatment centers exists. There are positive benefits to this clustering in the Twin Cities. Obviously, treatment is readily available for those individuals and families who are seeking help. Most of the centers have long waiting lists, and the waiting time fluctuates during the course of the year. This clustering has also provided direct benefits for program and treatment development. New techniques, new approaches to treatment, and programmatic approaches to recovery are developed within the treatment centers. Cross-fertilization occurs. Although independently organized and managed, this cluster of treatment centers tends to increase the sophistication and competency of all staffs and programs.

But again, there is no need to reinvent the wheel. The pressure ought not to be for the creation of additional clusters of treatment centers. Efforts must be in the direction of providing a balanced coverage of treatment centers on a geographical and population basis.

St. Mary's is definitely committed to the continued development of its treatment and to the development of treatment centers in other areas of this country. We know the solutions to the problems of chemical dependency do not lie exclusively in working with treatment, as the entire purpose of treatment is reactive to an already present problem. If our society puts its major effort solely into treatment, then we have not even begun to approach resolutions of the problems related to chemical dependency.

After-the-fact care and concern are not enough. The personal, social, and financial consequences of chemical dependency are too severe if we rely almost exclusively on treatment. The personal and social consequences of chemical dependency are too costly, however measured, to the chemically dependent individual, other family members, and the organizations of which that individual is a member. Increased emphasis must be given to the development of responsible prevention programs and methodologies.

Within the world of chemical dependency workers, there is a lot of discussion about prevention. What is it? What steps can be taken to develop prevention efforts? What are we preventing? How will you know if prevention efforts are successful? These questions and others equally serious and difficult must receive attention for serious and responsible prevention efforts to be realized.

The development of a comprehensive prevention program must take into account the various ways our society has dealt with the chemically dependent individual and the various issues surrounding chemical dependency. It is not as though we are starting with a chalkboard on which nothing is written. A vast amount of activity has occurred in the past that affects the way people are going to respond to any truly preventive measures.

We live in a society that endorses the use of mood-altering chemicals. The promotion and sale of mood-altering chemicals is big business in this country. Millions of dollars are spent annually to advertise the so-called benefits of alcoholic beverages, tobacco, and all of the over-the-counter, nonprescriptive medications. Not only is there a cultural mindset that endorses the use of mood-altering chemicals to make life easier, but there is a mindset in our culture that encourages the medication of our moods and feelings. It is a rare magazine or newspaper that does not carry advertisements selling the virtues of chemicals to "make life better." Although television and radio do not carry advertisements for distilled alcoholic beverages (e.g., whiskey, bourbon, Scotch), beer, wine, and other forms of legal nonprescriptive mood-altering chemicals are advertised, described, and pushed as the answer to loneliness, tension, pain, and self-improvement. According to the advertisements, beer and wine make social occasions even better.

Our culture endorses easy ways to avoid dealing with personal problems. It is relatively inexpensive and very easy to take an aspirin compound to medicate headache symptoms, to purchase a six-pack of beer, medicate our mood, and not feel for a while our anxieties and tensions. Our culture endorses the temporary and the continued medication of emotional pain. It is almost as though symptom relief is an American right. The risk and potential danger in symptom relief is that people do not pay attention to the problems causing the pain; rather, they seek immediate relief from the symptoms.

This attitude is just as prevalent for prescriptive medications as it is for nonprescriptive compounds. When people hurt, they go to a physican for treatment, and most often they go expecting some immediate relief from their pain. The drive and motivation is not to care for the physical or emotional condition that precipitates the pain;

it is to eliminate the pain. However, if people experience physical or emotional pain, it is because something is wrong within their bodies or their lives.

Being uncomfortable is a symptom that something is wrong. As such, discomfort is a signal and a message. The logical response is to pay attention to the message and take the steps to correct what is wrong. However, we live in a culture that endorses modifying the discomfort message so we don't receive it. The problems will continue; the physical or emotional pain signals will be present; but the medicated brain will prevent the reception of those signals. If people do not experience discomfort, they don't have to pay attention to the problem causing the feelings of discomfort.

This culture also contains an effective double-bind regarding the medication of discomfort. On the one hand, medication and discomfort relief is endorsed and encouraged. On the other hand, our culture penalizes those individuals who become chemically dependent as a result of medicating discomfort. Ultimately, this punitive approach denies the fact that continued medication does change the chemistry and the function of the brain and results in chemical dependency and, eventually, physical addiction. When this occurs, the chemically dependent individual is penalized as being weak, immoral, irresponsible, morally corrupt. To penalize the chemically dependent indivudal is to deny the reality that chemicals will eventually control the behavior of the individual, that the chemicals will eventually generate behavior destructive to the individual and those people surrounding the chemically dependent person.

The punitive approach is based on the assumption that chemically dependent people are still in control of their lives; that these individuals choose to ruin their lives and therefore must be penalized for it. This approach is not logical; it is not based on any sound understanding of chemical dependency, but it is nonetheless prevalent and real. "She would be a good mother if she would just stop drinking and love her husband and children." "He has such good parents and such a loving wife, but he is certainly an irresponsible husband to keep drinking the way he does." "He was a very good student, but he just doesn't care anymore, he'd rather run with that gang of kids and smoke pot." Comments such as these are spoken every day. It is easier to condemn someone as immoral and irresponsible than it is to be logical and intervene in the process of chemical dependency, to work for the reestablishment of a healthy individual.

There is a second major problem in our society regarding chemical dependency If someone does begin the recovery process, if a person does experience recovery through treatment, that individual will carry the stigma of being an ex-junkie or an ex-alcoholic. It becomes more difficult to apply for life insurance, health insurance, driver's licenses, and employment. The individual is now subject to potential penalties for taking care of himself or herself. People know they will probably be penalized for seeking treatment, and the penalties they pay are real and severe. For instance, an airline pilot who has successfully completed treatment and is effectively maintaining sobriety will have extreme difficulty regaining a position in the company and the approval of federal agencies. Our present social system encourages people to not deal with chemical dependency problems.

21 Past Attempts To Prevent Chemical Dependency

Our society has a history of attempting to control chemical abuse as well as attempting to reduce the prevalence of chemical abuse (that is, early steps in prevention). There have been five distinct generations of measures to control and reduce chemical dependency since the end of Prohibition; each is still present and active. Each has been developed in response to the personal and social consequences of chemical dependency. Each has contributed strengths and weaknesses to succeeding generations. Comprehensive efforts toward prevention of chemical dependency must take into account the movement and dynamics of each of these generations, because each in its own way has contributed to the current dynamics operating within our society.

Phase I

The end of Prohibition placed heavy reliance on the legal system of this country for control of chemical abuse. Control was now centered in the laws, law enforcement, and the court system. State and federal statutes defined responsible use. If alcohol could not be prohibited, at least it could be controlled. These controls determined a minimum

approach a discussion of the types of legal drugs that most people were using. During the 1960s, schools that inaugurated these types of programs frequently experienced an increase in chemical usage not a decrease.

Phase III

This generation evolved from the previous one. It is also an educational approach, but one easily distinguishable from the scare tactic. Serious questions were raised about the effectiveness of the previous educational approach. Public opinion surveys and scientific research indicated that experimentation and continued use of mood-altering chemicals were unaffected by the scare tactic. In an attempt to modify the educational approach, a generation of drug education was initiated that tried to present the facts as they are known.

This educational approach attempted to correct the messages previously communicated. Throughout the educational system and the youth groups of our religious systems, new forms of drug education appeared. Factual information about chemicals was disseminated through the use of speakers, printed material, and films. There was a conscious effort to not tell the audience what they should do. It was assumed that if all of the information were known, the individual would make the right choice, that is, not to abuse mood-altering chemicals. This informational approach gained widespread acceptance, and a generation of high school students has grown up in this country under its influence.

Phase IV

By 1970, the search for improvements in preventative drug education had evolved into yet a new form. Research in the process of chemical dependency and experience in the treatment of chemical dependency identified what appeared to be a major factor in differences between chemically dependent persons and the nonchemically dependent user of mood-altering substances.

It had been known for some time that successful treatment resulted in the reestablishment of a personal sense of values. Successful treatment required giving serious attention to the development and strengthening of personal value systems. Workers within the field of chemical dependency, especially those involved with education, began to design and implement preventive drug education seminars that focused on the relationship between chemical use and personal values. Many institutions developed their own curriculum within this approach. School systems, religious bodies, and social service agencies initiated this generation of preventive drug education.

An example of this approach is the Values Clarification Program developed by the Metropolitan YMCA of Akron, Ohio. Their approach utilizes trained group workers, films, and written material to stimulate discussions on personal decision making and values. This approach is based on the assumption that small groups of people (children, adolescents, and adults) can examine their behavior and base the choice to use or not use mood-altering chemicals on their own sense of personal values. This approach strongly emphasizes the need for personal decisions and for continued clarifications and development of personal value systems.

Phase V

Within the last few years, there has appeared an organized approach to chemical dependency treatment and prevention within the business and industrial sector of our society. This approach, appearing under several names, is best described as an employee assistance program. It is basically an early intervention program. The idea is to be able to identify people in the work force who are having difficulty with chemical dependency and get them into treatment as early as possible.

To be effective, this type of program relies heavily on the presence of four conditions:

1. The program must have the endorsement and support of top leadership within management and labor.

2. Supervisory personnel must be skilled in identifying possible chemically dependent behavior.

3. There must be extensive diagnostic capability, and there must be competent treatment available if chemical dependency is diagnosed.

4. Company policy and the social climate must endorse the disease concept of chemical dependency, must encourage treatment as a positive step toward recovery, and must remove the stigma and penalties so frequently associated with the diagnosis of chemical dependency.

St. Mary's is working with employers in the development and sophistication of this approach. We offer extensive diagnostic capability and a competent treatment program. It has been our experience that where employers will conscientiously work to incorporate this approach as a part of personnel benefits, where employers will work to construct a social climate conducive to early intervention, then an employee assistance program is effective for both employers and employees. Conversely, it is also our experience that where employers initiate such an approach without constructing positive personnel policies and without attempting to modify the negative social climate, this approach is not effective within that company and the employee assistance program may be counterproductive; the program will be seen as a way to penalize alcoholics.

Efforts to construct a truly preventive program must take into account the heritage of the five generations of chemical control. They are the precursors, the forerunners of any efforts now undertaken. The attitudes and the mindsets of our population have been formed from the experience of one or a combination of these generations. Some people believe the only way to prevent chemical abuse is to write tougher laws, strengthen our police departments, and require mandatory penalties upon conviction. Others will argue just as rigorously that a mandatory form of drug education is the only way to approach the problem of chemical dependency. Still another group will argue that we must strengthen personal character through moral and religious persuasion.

At St. Mary's, we believe that prevention must be approached from a different perspective. We find no evidence to indicate that educators or religious leaders have some inherent characteristic that provides them immunity from chemical dependency. It is our belief that prevention efforts must be consistent with what is known about why people use mood-altering chemicals and about the process of chemical dependency. We must link this base of information with the insights and learning gained from the experience of successfully treating thousands of people.

The design of prevention efforts requires a very deliberate and conscientious examination of mood-altering chemicals, the patterns of usage, the identification of destructive usage patterns, and the development of an approach to intervene in the lives of individuals before the usage pattern becomes destructive.

The remaining portion of this book describes our approach to the prevention of the disease of alcoholism. What is said about the prevention of alcoholism is equally true for the prevention of dependency on the other mood-altering chemicals.

22 Identifying Drinking Patterns

It is important to distinguish the various types of drinking patterns. Some drinking patterns are nondestructive, others are destructive to the individual and to the individual's family. Prevention of alcoholism does not necessarily mean total abstinence. Efforts to prevent alcoholism will differentiate among drinking patterns and will work to inhibit and deter destructive dependent drinking. The following typology is useful in identifying the kinds of drinking that will be the subject of prevention efforts.

Drinking Patterns

Nondestructive and nondependent	Characterized by:
• Diversion, relaxation, • entertainment drinking • Ritualistic drinking • "Time-out" drinking	• Relatively small amounts • No toxic state developed • No harmful side effects • Pleasant experience • Positive experience • Positive feeling state

Figure 12

There are at least three types of drinking patterns that are nondestructive and nondependent (see Figure 12). All three types are prevalent in our society, and many people will participate in these types of drinking patterns without experiencing any harmful effects.

The first type is the kind of drinking that occurs for relaxation and entertainment. This drinking patterns ranges all the way from having a beer at the bowling alley to enjoying wine or cocktails at a party.

The second type is ritualistic, meaning that the drinking pattern is directly associated with an event, and the drinking of alcoholic beverages is a part of the ritual accompanying that event. This may be represented by a glass of wine with a meal, or by the pitcher of beer that is on the dinner table in many homes. It may have religious significance, such as wine served at a religious celebration.

The third type is simply the "time-out" drinking. This can be represented by having a beer on a very hot day after you have mowed the grass or by having a beer or a cocktail after a hard day's work.

These types of nondestructive and nondepdendent drinking patterns share common characteristics. Relatively small amounts of alcohol will be consumed. In each of the three types, the individual will have one or two drinks, will feel refreshed and relaxed, and will not drink more. The drinking will be a pleasant and positive experience, and alcohol will not be consumed to the point of developing a toxic state.

Drinking Patterns

Destructive or dependent	Characterized by:
• Stress drinking	• Intoxication
• Problem drinking	• Relatively large amounts
• Addictive drinking	• Harmful side effects
	• Unpleasant experience
	• Negative experience
	• Negative feeling state

Figure 13

There are at least three destructive or dependent types of drinking (see Figure 13). These drinking patterns are distinctly different from nondestructive drinking.

The first type is stress or situational drinking. Typically, the individual who follows this type of drinking pattern is constantly living in a high-stress state of mind and will reduce the experience of that stress by constantly using alcohol. Other individuals will experience intermittent periods of high stress and will drink abusively at those times. These individuals will cease abusive drinking when the stress recedes.

For example, consider two people going to the same party. One individual has two drinks, enjoys the party, and goes home with a pleasant experience of socializing with friends. The second person, experiencing high levels of stress, goes to the same party, continues drinking until a toxic state develops, and returns home believing that the best thing about the party was the alcoholic beverage. The first person has participated in a nondestructive and nondependent drinking pattern. The second person, if operating under a great deal of stress, has exhibited a destructive and dependent drinking pattern.

Another type of destructive or dependent drinking is problem drinking. In outward appearance this type of drinking appears very much like stress drinking, but there are differences. There is no demonstrable crisis to account for the stress. The problems and the stress are pervasive and not related to a particular event. Such individuals will drink in order to escape their problems and to reduce the mental pain associated with those problems.

The third type of destructive drinking is addictive drinking. Physical or psychological addiction or both is present in this person's life, and the individual has no control over the amount consumed.

These three types of destructive or dependent drinking have a common set of characteristics. Frequently the individuals will drink relatively large amounts of alcohol and will drink to intoxication. The drinking experience has harmful side effects, and the negative experiences will eventually erode the individual's ability to function emotionally, socially, intellectually, spiritually, and physically. Destructive and dependent drinking behavior produces negative results, inducing a negative feeling state within the individual.

On the basis of our work at St. Mary's, we have defined what we consider to be a prototype or profile of an individual who will not enter into abusive drinking patterns with alcohol. The developing work on social competencies is consistent with one aspect of this prototypic profile. We believe the individual who does not (and will not) enter into abusive drinking patterns with alcohol has five basic characteristics, which are outlined below.

1. *The individual will have a well-defined and livable value system.* The individual will be able to say "These are the things I believe about life," "These are the principles upon which I will base my behavior," and "This is what I will do and this is what I won't do." The individual develops the understanding that value systems are constantly being

refined. The individual will not be perfectionistic, will not expect to be right and error-free all the time. Rather, the individual will have incorporated into his or her value system the understanding that all are fallible human beings. The individual will have incorporated into the value system ways to handle feelings of guilt.

2. *The individual will have a well-developed self-image.* This self-image will be based in reality; it will not be deceptive or blown out of proportion. The individual will feel good about self. There will be a realistic assessment of abilities. The individual will have well-defined boundaries, knowing where self ends and others begin.

3. *The individual will possess the ability to develop stable, mature, healthy, intimate relationships with other people.* The individual will experience pain and frustration within these relationships but will constantly keep in mind that intimate relationships are also health producing. The individual will have the experience of an intimate relationship(s) in which he or she will give and receive acceptance and love.

4. *The individual will experience tolerable amounts of anxiety, depression, and guilt feelings.* These feelings will not be debilitating or destructive. The individual will know that he or she is not unique in experiencing those feelings. The individual will expect to experience anxiety, depression, and guilty feelings and will have developed ways to resolve them.

5. *The individual will experience the presence of coping mechanisms, developed to the level that the individual can deal with reality.* The individual will have a sense of how to struggle with hard times.

These characteristis may not apply to the individual who experiences a genetic or metabolic predisposition to alcoholism. If this predisposition is present, it may override these characteristics of personal strength.

Prevention efforts must be directed toward the development of these five characteristics. Prevention will include very specific, intentionally planned activities that will enhance and enable the growth of these characteristics within individuals. Prevention is not generalized activity under the name of drug education. Rather, prevention activities are those activities that promote the healthy growth of the human personality to incorporate these five characteristics.

Prevention is a systematic and well-coordinated approach to the development of human beings who have a well-defined, livable value system and a well-developed self-image, who possess intimate relationships, who experience only tolerable amounts of emotional pain, and who have coping mechanisms developed to deal with reality (see Figure 14, Summary Table on the development of these competencies).

Work toward developing prevention efforts is now underway in many places. Many agencies serving youth are introducing into their programming efforts aimed at the prevention of alcoholism among youth. Further, many state and local governmental units have now created offices for chemical dependency prevention. The National Institute of Alcohol Abuse and Alcoholism is working through its national and regional offices to support prevention efforts. Although these initial efforts have taken many forms and are conducted under differing lines of authority and accountability (social agencies and governmental units), all have a basic approach in common. Each in its own way is attemptintg to promote healthy growth of individuals and, in so doing, intends to discourage the use of alcohol as a way to solve problems or to avoid personal problems. In the language of one state chemical dependency prevention office, efforts must pay close attention to the factors that influence the development of social competencies. These social competencies are summarized in Figure 14.

SUMMARY TABLE*

Factors Which Influence the Development of the Social Competencies

Trust	Self-Confidence	Directionality
Developing trust in family relationships	Encouraging the development of capabilities through family support	Socializing into a set of purposeful values
Developing trust in peer group relationships	Being aware of capabilities	Identifying with reference individuals who have a meaningful purpose in life
Interacting cooperatively with others	Using capabilities successfully in cooperative, competitive and individual situations	Being aware of family and peer models

*Devoloped by David W. Johnson, Professor of Educational Psychology, University of Minnesota. Published in *A Minnesota Primer of the Prevention of Chemical Use Problems*, Minnesota Alcohol and Drug Authority, September 1976, pp. 12–13.

SUMMARY TABLE (cont'd)

Trust	Self-Confidence	Directionality
Developing trust skills	Receiving recognition and approval from family and peers for successful use of capabilities	Understanding of one's values
	Developing the interpersonal skills needed for risking disclosure of capabilities and accurately receiving positive feedback from family and peers	Exploring of potential interest Experiencing cooperative effort towards valued goals
Identity	**Perspective Taking**	**Interpersonal Skills**
Identifying with individuals of emotional significance	Taking the perspective of other people and viewing oneself as they view one	Being able to socialize with groups of valued people
Identifying with reference groups		Training in specific skills
Receiving esteem from valued people	Interacting cooperatively with others	Interacting cooperatively with others
Developing values	Training in judgmental stage development	
Comparing oneself to others in cooperative, competitive, and individualistic situations	Exposure to heterogenity in people and situations	
Increasing self-awareness through feedback from others	Training in sending and receiving appropriate messages	
Increasing awareness of peer group values		

Figure 14

This developing work on social competencies fits very well into an understanding of prevention that views the human personality holistically, believing that the prevention of alcoholism and other forms of chemical dependency must work with all aspects of the human personality.

23 Why Drink Destructively?

If dependent or destructive drinking is so negative and produces such negative results within an individual, why do people continue to drink destructively? The development of prevention efforts will take into account why people drink destructively. On the basis of the treatment experience of St. Mary's, there are at least eleven possible responses to this question. Words of caution are needed at this point. Keep in mind that alcoholics will rationalize and create excuses for their drinking pattern. The following material is not the response of such rationalizing and excuse making.

1. It appears that some individuals are genetically predisposed to destructive drinking. These individuals will frequently drink destructively once they begin to consume alcohol not because they want to, but because it is a part of their genetic makeup. Research continues to discover further information and to better understand this genetic predisposition. There is research that indicates this genetic predisposition is present in a cross-section of our population.

2. A very small percentage of our population have a physical condition that produces abnormal metabolizing of alcohol within the body. In these cases, the body simply does not metabolize alcohol in the usual manner, and so it is common for these people to have unusual or negative experiences associated with the consumption of alcohol.

3. Some people will eventually enter destructive drinking patterns because of preexisting physical or mental illnesses. It is not uncommon for an individual to begin a heavy drinking pattern as a result of

illness. For example, some individuals suffering acute mental depression will engage in destructive drinking patterns; some people suffering severe physical illness will initiate periods of heavy drinking in response to the discomfort they experience as a result of the illness.

4. Many of the people who enter St. Mary's treatment programs were children in homes where heavy drinking was a pattern for one or both of the parents. In some cases, the parents themselves were alcoholics, though in other cases they were not. The parent or parents modeled behavior that included heavy drinking. Parents who drink heavily tend to produce the same behavior within their children. A large percentage of these children experiencing problems with drinking are probably giving evidence of the previously described genetic predisposition. This is particularly true of male children. There is a large category of people entering treatment who grew up as children with an alcoholic parent or parents.

5. Interestingly enough, another large category of people entering treatment grew up in homes where parents practiced total abstinence from all alcoholic beverages. There are three negative factors that seem to influence these children as they begin to drink as adolescents or adults.

First of all, they were raised in homes where there was no parental role of moderate and responsible consumption of alcohol. They have not learned from the adults most significant in their lives how to responsibly approach the consumption of alcohol.

Second, when these individuals begin to drink as adolescents or adults, they do so with a great deal of guilt. Many people who practice total abstinence do so with a great deal of moral pride, and this moral position is conveyed to the chiildren. When the children begin to drink, one of the natural outcomes is the feeling of guilt. Some people are not able to handle the guilt they feel related to drinking, and a spiraling effect begins.

Third, there is frequently a great deal of moral rigidity accompanying total abstinence. People who grow up within a morally rigid home frequently do not develop the flexibility necessary to successfully cope with reality. They do not develop the ability to accommodate themselves to changing and challenging situations. During adolescence, many of these children will rebel, reject this moral rigidity and begin drinking. If the drinking is excessive and large amounts of guilt are experienced, it is easy for such individuals, to slip into the spiraling effects of chemical dependency.

6. There was much material presented in the first section of this

book concerning coping skills. Some people enter into destructive drinking patterns because their coping skills are not adequate to get them through the "rough spots." The level of coping skills varies from individual to individual. Alcoholic beverages are initially effective in reducing the experienced pain when an individual is in a situation over his or her head. After the initial effects, the continued use of alcoholic beverages will eventually diminish coping skills, causing more experienced pain and the continued use of drinking.

7. A pervasive sense of loneliness and self-isolation can result in increased drinking, which, in turn, can result in the development of destructive drinking patterns. Some people never experience intimate relationships with other people. The loss of intimate relationships will frequently precipitate destructive drinking. The experience of loneliness can become so powerful that individuals can turn to the consumption of alcohol as a way to modify and dull the emotional pain.

8. A likely candidate for destructive drinking is the individual with little self-confidence. These individuals typically will have a very low image of themselves, they will constantly seek the approval of other people, they do not believe in themselves. Consumption of alcohol is one way to initially attain a state of well-being, to feel better about oneself. Eventually, the destructive drinking pattern will remove this pleasant sense of well-being, but the individual perceives no other way to get through the day.

9. Some people enter a destructive drinking pattern as a way to deal with an intolerable stress level. For any number of reasons, the individual has come up against a situation that has produced an intolerable stress level. The stress is not short lived, but spans a period of time. The consumption of alcoholic beverages is initiated to dull the experience of stress and gradually develops into destructive drinking behavior.

10. Everyone faces anxiety; everyone must cope throughout life with anxiety-producing situations. Each of us copes with anxiety in different ways. As the anxiety level increases, each of us must find ways to behave that will reduce the level of anxiety we experience. If our behavior is ineffective in reducing anxiety, or if the anxiety level is of such a magnitude as to exceed our tolerance level, then new ways of coping have to be discovered. Some people discover that alcohol is a very effective modifier of experienced anxiety. It is quite possible for such individuals to gradually move from moderate drinking to a

destructive drinking pattern, especially if they have learned no alternate behavior that will lead to the reduction of anxiety.

11. The presence of an overwhelming sense of shame and guilt can become an intolerable state of mind. Many people who experience these feelings turn to the use of alcoholic beverages to modify and examine what is an intolerable feeling state. This sense of shame and guilt may be the result of previous behaviors and actions or it may be an overreaction and blown out of proportion. In either case, the individual cannot tolerate for long periods of time the pervasive and deepening sense of guilt. Initially, the consumption of alcohol will induce a sense of well-being and a state of mind that permits the individual to escape from the guilt feelings. Ultimately, however, the behaviors resulting from destructive drinking will produce additional feelings of shame and guilt. Rather than resolving shame and guilt, drinking will produce greater feelings of shame and guilt, and the downward spiral of chemical dependency is in effect.

There is no single answer to the question, "Why do people drink destructively?" The eleven characteristics described are the most common we see in the people who come to St. Mary's for treatment. Generally, a combination of these characteristics will be present within an individual. Just as the human personality is very complex, so also are the precipitating factors that lead to destructive drinking.

24 Goals of Prevention

Prevention efforts must take into account the personal and social factors that influence the development of destructive drinking patterns. Based on observation and the experience of working with those people who do become alcoholic drinkers, prevention efforts must develop approaches to eliminate the individual need for destructive drinking. To be effective, these approaches must enhance and further peoples' capacity to find meaning in their lives, to develop and sustain stable and mature intimate relationships, and to develop coping skills for dealing with reality.

Much of the discussion taking place today within the world of chemical dependency workers concerns the definition of prevention. Much time and energy is spent in both discussion and argument to clarify the meaning of prevention. Prevention efforts must be directed toward three groupings of people within this society:

1. The population of people who run a strong risk of chemical dependency; for example, chemical dependency exists in other members of their family.

2. The population experiencing problems with drinking who are not yet alcoholic and in whom the detrimental effects are not quite so severe.

3. The population of the young who have not yet embarked upon the use of chemicals.

Although there are some people who say that prevention must be restricted to the third population, it is quite appropriate to develop and implement prevention programs designed for all three populations.

What are appropriate and responsible goals for prevention? What can be done to reduce and eventually prevent the destructive use of mood-altering chemicals? What can our society and our institutions do to enable people to live without entering the process of chemical dependency? Although the answers to these questions appear to be very complex, there are direct and straightforward actions that can be initiated in the name of prevention. The goals of prevention are outlined below:

1. Prevention efforts will produce an internal state whereby individuals are able to make a free choice to drink or not to drink. Individuals will choose according to their value systems and also according to their assessment of the situation. Crucial to the fulfillment of this goal are the phrases *free choice* and *to drink or not to drink.* Peer pressure and social expectations will have diminished influence on the individual's choice.

2. Prevention efforts will offer realistic alternatives to drinking. The individual and groups of people must experience the positive benefits of socializing without the use of alcohol. These efforts will result in individuals' understanding and desiring to experience reality in a nonmedicated state of mind.

3. Prevention efforts will enable individuals to drink in a nonabusive, nondestructive fashion. Many people, exercising their free choice, will elect to consume alcoholic beverages. Prevention efforts will aid individuals to understand, experience, and desire responsible use. All drinking is not abusive; all drinking is not destructive. Prevention efforts must be as responsive to those who choose to drink as it is to those who choose not to drink.

4. Prevention efforts will develop a system where current abusive use (nonalcoholic) can be reduced to nonabusive, nondestructive usage patterns. There are many people in our society who are currently abusing alcohol, although they are not yet involved in the descending spiral of chemical dependency. Prevention efforts will be directed to aid these people so that they can back away from abusive and destructive drinking patterns.

5. Prevention efforts will offer a quality of life that is achievable without the consumption of alcoholic beverages. The mythologies and false statements contained in the advertisements of alcoholic beverages need to be stripped away. The real man or woman, the

sophisticated man or woman, does not have to drink alcoholic beverages. In fact, qualities of life currently ascribed to drinking are false and cannot be achieved. Femininity, masculinity, sociability, and meaningful relationships with others are not produced by the consumption of alcohol. Prevention efforts will offer opportunities for personal growth and development that are nonchemically oriented and are not achievable through the consumption of alcohol.

6. Prevention efforts will offer opportunities for the development of a personal system of priorities and values. Individuals will be clearer about what they believe and about what they will do. There will be clarity about what is important and what is unimportant.

7. Prevention efforts will offer opportunities for the development of a personal understanding of fulfillment. Individuals will be clearer about the kind of life they want to live. On the basis of a personal sense of value and priority, individuals will be able to choose actions and behaviors that will be directed toward fulfillment of their potential.

8. Prevention efforts will provide a system of education describing the ultimate physical, social, emotional, intellectual, and spiritual effects resulting from the use of mood-altering chemicals. Unfortunately, most education today has not attempted to view the individual as a totality but has centered on the physical and legal consequences resulting from the use of mood-altering chemicals. These efforts have ignored the emotional, intellectual, social, and spiritual effects. Prevention efforts will offer a basic understanding of alcoholism and the addictive process. This basic understanding must incorporate all facets and aspects of the individual.

9. Prevention efforts will present a variety of modalities for dealing with anxiety, depression, and other unpleasant feeling states.

10. Prevention efforts will offer insights into the development of interpersonal relationships. A pervasive sense of loneliness exists within our society. Prevention efforts will counter this state of loneliness by offering opportunities for building skills leading to the development of relationships that provide support and love.

11. Prevention efforts will offer insights into the individual's relationship to self, others, and God. These efforts will be directed to how people view reality and understand life, and where self, others, and God fit into that world view.

25 New Directions in Prevention Efforts

Where can the kind of effort that has been described be initiated? Where can this kind of approach to prevention be initiated? Wherever prevention efforts can be initiated, St. Mary's places strong emphasis on working with those people who are in the helping professions. Rather than developing a new level of chemical dependency workers, rather than creating a new profession, it is more important that work be undertaken to further develop existing organizations and existing leadership so that they will incorporate into their work an understanding and a sensitivity to the characteristics of the chemically dependent person. There are four institutions within this country with which all people have some contact during their lives. These four are: the education system, the social service system, the religious system, and the health-care system.

These four systems have several characteristics in common. First, professionals within these systems work daily with people, many of whom are presently experiencing personal problems. Second, each system requires training and certification for admittance into its professional positions. Third, each system has a form of continuing education for its members. Fourth, there exists the possibility (and in some cases the reality) of interagency referral. Fifth, each generally experiences a long-term relationship with its clients.

Prevention must impact the personnel within each of these systems. Prevention efforts will address the specific ways in which personnel within these systems can influence and provide direction for clients (see Figure 15).

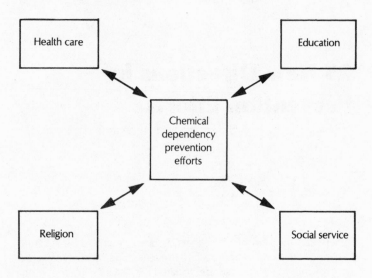

Figure 15

The Educational System

More people have contact with the educational system than with any other present nationwide system. The educational system has the obvious relationship with all children and youth. It also is one of the nation's larger employers. Further, within the last few years, efforts in continuing education have mushroomed to the point that many adults are now involved in evening courses in the public and parochial school systems. Most community education programs include courses related to family life and improvement of interpersonal relationships. Most school systems provide counseling and social work services to students and families, many at the local school level.

All of these factors support the viewpoint that the educational system has more contact with children and their families than any other system in this country. It is the single most important system having daily contact with the largest number of family members. In addition, there is a general mindset in this country that prevention is an educational effort. Chemical dependency prevention efforts should build on this attitude and strengthen efforts already existing within the educational system.

The educational process should incorporate an illustration of alternative lifestyles that can be the basis for students to develop effective living skills. The educational system has the delivery system and personnel to assist students in:

1. developing personality skills that will enrich (a.) child–child relationships, (b.) child–parent relationships, (c.) child–other adult relationships, and (d.) sibling relationships. Such learning does not have to be the content of any particular course; rather, throughout the primary and secondary grade levels, these social skills should be emphasized as part of the methodology and within the context of existing formalized instruction.

2. establishing a personally internalized value system. The goal is for students to develop a value system that clearly delineates beliefs as the basis for decision making and action.

3. presenting lifestyles that are free from the misuse and abuse of mood-altering substances. This can be accomplished by the behavior and role modeling of the adults within the educational system as well as by being incorporated into the development of value systems.

4. differentiating between use and abuse of mood-altering chemicals. Incorporated within personal value systems should be understanding and attitudes related to the question of total abstinence or responsible use. It is not the purpose of the educational system to predetermine which stance is most appropriate for the individual.

5. understanding the pharmacology of mood-altering chemicals and their physiological and psychological effects. This type of instruction should not be seen as a panacea to solve the drug problem existing in our school systems. Rather, this appraoch would require a straightforward presentation of the types of mood-altering chemicals used and abused, a detailed explanation of their physiological effects, and a comprehensive discussion of why and how these chemicals are capable and effective in altering the mood of anyone who uses them.

6. developing coping skills that would help students to deal with reality. This emphasis has as its goal enabling people to deal with life situations that threaten their equilibrium.

7. recognizing and managing personal stress. Much of the abuse of mood-altering chemicals centers around mismanagement of or inability to manage high levels of stress. The focus would be to assist people in reducing high levels of stress and better managing tolerable stress levels.

The majority of people who today are suffering the disease of chemical dependency began using mood-altering chemicals during their adolescent years. The early development of chemical dependency occurs, for most people, at the junior and senior high school levels. The school system is the major institution that has daily contact with both adolescents and their families. Thus it must have an appropriate role in any prevention efforts that are to be ultimately effective. There are many school administrators and many educational professionals who will reject this view, with support from a small percentage of the general population.

However, the majority of the population, the majority of school administrators, and many educational professionals are willing to participate in efforts to reduce chemical dependency. These people clearly understand the very important role that can be carried by the educational system. They are willing to learn and to employ their professional skills in the development of courses and an educational environment in which chemical dependency prevention efforts can be implemented.

Without great difficulty, courses can be developed and presented as a part of the postgraduate education for existing educational professionals. Most school systems require in-service training for their employees. Any local school board, administration, and organization of school employees could develop over a very short time the ways to include all the emphases necessary for truly effective prevention efforts. Highly motivated professionals already exist within our school systems, individuals who are ready and willing to provide direction and guidance in these efforts. Any additional training that is needed or required should be obtainable through postgraduate education. There should be a cooperative effort between the educational systems and chemical dependency treatment centers to construct the educational and training opportunities that will result in prevention efforts.

The Social Service System

Included in this category are the public and private agencies that provide social services, such as the YWCA, the YMCA, Boy Scouts, Girl Scouts, mental health associations, senior citizens' associations, community agencies, and so on. These types of organizations must be involved in efforts to prevent chemical dependency. They can present the following types of programs and services:

1. The presentation of lifestyles free from chemical abuse. People of all ages need to understand that there are alternative ways of living, ways that do not include the necessity for use of mood-altering chemicals.

2. The presentation of factual material related to the physiological and pharmacological properties of mood-altering chemicals. This type of program does not need to be relegated solely to the educational system. The community social service agencies can just as well incorporate this into their programming.

3. The development of interpersonal communications skills. Our population must have the opportunity to participate in events that increase communication of feelings, attitudes, and beliefs. Social service agencies can provide this opportunity for a large number of people who do not have contact with the religious systems, who have limited contact with the health-care systems, and who may have no contact with the educational systems.

4. The development of interpersonal relationships. Many agencies have this emphasis as one of their central programming goals. The public has a right to expect that agencies will provide the experiences that will result in learning how to develop and systain interpersonal relationships that provide support and love.

5. The provision of courses and experiences that will enable people to better handle anxiety, anger, depression, and stress.

The Religious System

Every parish, every local congregation should have available a well-developed system for enabling members and neighborhood residents to live more effective lives. These efforts would be found in both counseling and teaching. There should be a very well-defined approach to the development of integrated, ''whole'' people. The religious system must develop ways for people to understand and experience the authentic relationship between God, self, and others. The religious system of this country should have a very significant role in providing the tools that will enable people to live with day-to-day frustrations and crises.

1. Certainly the religious system should provide the counseling and teaching that will enable people to develop nonconflicting value systems. This does not mean that all people will live harmoniously. Efforts in chemical dependency prevention are not based on this kind of daydreaming. The goal is for individuals to develop and experience

personal value systems that are in and of themselves, as free of conflict as possible. Individuals should be able to express what they believe, what they will and won't do, and should be able to base personal action on well-defined beliefs.

2. There must be individual and group ways to resolve guilt. These efforts must go far beyond prayers of confession and words of absolution. People must experience forgiveness and be able to move away from the crippling effects of guilt. The religious system must offer effective ways for people to cope with their guilt, to learn how to resolve guilt, and to experience the release from guilt through forgiveness.

3. A large number of people who abuse mood-altering chemicals do so in their reactions to grief situations. The religious system must develop more effective ways of enabling people to constructively cope with grief and to experience support and not be left to endure their grief in loneliness.

4. Stress is a major factor in the development of many illnesses. Local pastors, rabbis, and laity have the opportunity to develop and implement programs and activities that will result in peoples' learning to reduce and manage stress.

5. Most religious groupings view themselves as providing fellowship and a sense of community. Therefore, they should provide ways for people to develop fulfilling interpersonal relationships. They should be teaching people ways to live together, ways to develop interpersonal realtionships that will provide support and the experience of being loved. These efforts should reduce the sense of alienation existing in this country.

6. The religious system must expand its efforts to increase communication skills. Human beings are social creatures. The degree to which individuals can communicate with clarity and precision is the degree to which they will effectively relate with others. Clarity of communication does not require a highly sophisticated vocabulary. It does require the ability to identify and express specific feelings, attitudes, and beliefs.

Members of local congregations and parishes have the right to expect that their particular religious organizaion will offer leadership training that will make these kinds of programs a present reality in the life of the congregation. This leadership training should be conducted for both the ordained clergy and the laity. It should be a part of the regular curriculum of all seminaries and a part of the postgraduate and continuing education offered within the religious system. Clergy ought to be able to identify and recognize chemically dependent people who come to them with a variety of personal problems. Clergy should not be timid in confronting parishioners who are exhibiting chemical dependent behavior.

Seminaries and congregations can readily work with chemical dependency treatment centers to provide educational opportunities that will expand prevention efforts.

The Health-Care System

Included within the health care system are M.D.s, nurses, psychologists, industrial health personnel and paraprofessionals. These professionals and paraprofessionals are found in private practice, clinics, hospitals, and industry. Historically, these people have exercised their skills in the role of healer. Deeply embedded in our society is the view that you go to a doctory if you're sick. Advances have generally come in the areas of surgical procedures, diagnostic techniques, and healing therapies. Without a doubt, all three areas are extremely important; much pain and suffering has been reduced or eliminated because of these advances.

Generally, however, *healer* is a more accurate description of the medical professional than is the *preventer*. Preventive medicine, though practiced by a few professionals, is not a major force within the health-care professions today. Dentistry has succeeded in its efforts to incorporate preventive medicine into the everyday work of most dentists, but dentistry stands alone. Within the world of the medical doctor, the annual physical is no longer receiving the emphasis once given this preventive measure. The growing emphasis given now to family and holistic medicine are steps in the right direction, but these trends are small and will not provide medical services to the majority of the population.

There are definite, specific steps the medical profession must take in order to participate in the needed emphasis for chemical dependency prevention. Within this profession are highly trained personnel, most of whom are receptive to additional training and could incorporate into existing practices these specific steps for chemical dependency prevention.

Initially, the health-care system and its professionals must reexamine the use of prescriptive medicines. We recognize the clear and legitimate need for psychotropic drugs in treating major physical and psychiatric problems. We place the emphasis here on *major* problems. All too often, members of the medical profession prescribe psychotropic drugs for illnesses that are not major. When this occurs, physicians are providing symptom relief not treatment for illness. The prescriptive use of barbiturates and tranquilizers is on the increase. The medical profession must begin acting in such a way that the use of prescriptive medicine is reserved for major illnesses and must offer treatment for minor illnesses and symptoms without psychotropic drugs.

In addition, the health-care system must work to establish preventive programs that are specifically designed to assist participants in developing and strengthening skills to cope with reality. These programs can be located within a private practice, a clinic, a hospital, or an industrial setting, or they may be created independently. In any case, the programs ought to be based on a holistic understanding of the human being.

There should be group teaching or counseling experiences where participants can learn:

1. ways to cope with anxiety. These experiences would strive to develop and strengthen coping skills related to anxiety reduction; they would also be aimed at aiding the participants in learning how to live with anxiety. Currently, patients are treated with tranquilizers; prevention calls for the development of coping skills and the reduction of anxiety in nonmedicated ways.

2. ways to cope with anger. The medical profession treats the results of anger turned inward as well as the results of anger turned outward, that is physical aggression. The illnesses and accidents resulting from anger are present in the physician's office. Physicians ought to have their patients participating in programs where they have the chance to learn how to appropriately cope with anger.

3. ways to cope with depression. Instead of prescribing psychotropic drugs routinely for depression, group teaching or counseling experiences would assist the patient in developing ways to cope with and minimize the effects of depression, thereby eliminating or diminishing the need for drugs for some patients.

4. alternative chemically free lifestyles. This is not a substitute for treatment; it is a course designed for the nonchemically dependent. The goal of these experiences is the reduction in personal use of psychotropic drugs, both prescriptive and nonprescriptive, including alcohol.

5. the development of ego strength. There must be experiential learning situations where participants can begin to increase their ego strength as one of the measures to prevent chemical dependency.

6. communications skills. It should be obvious that social beings need to communicate clearly and with precision in order to sustain a high quality of life. Many people need to learn or to increase their communications skills to effectively increase their interpersonal relationships.

7. dynamics of chemical dependency. These courses would provide basic information about the dynamics of chemical dependency: effects of psychotropic drugs on the body, personal capabilities, and interpersonal relationships.

8. ways to cope with stress. Many of the patients coming into the physician's office are struggling with stress; the stress is beginning to override their coping ability. These individuals ought to have the opportunity to develop and strengthen coping skills related to stress tolerance and reduction.

9. ways to develop health-producing relationships. Personal loneliness and isolation is a recurring theme in the physician's office. The medical profession ought to provide experiences for patients to develop interpersonal relationships as a way of developing healthy individuals.

10. ways to cope with grief. Grief therapy is all too often used only with those people unable to cope with grief after a prolonged period of time. At the occasion of grief, patients should have the opportunity and encouragement to enter immediately into group experiences designed specifically to assist them in coping with grief.

The health-care system and its professionals should be involved in the development and extension of biofeedback and meditation as two very specific techniques for teaching people to cope with reality. Both techniques can be taught in a variety of ways and both will provide immediate results to the participant.

The availability and utilization of individual and family counseling must be increased as a preventative effort. Physicians must increase their efforts in referral to competent counseling personnel. In order to accomplish this, physicians must be aware of the signs and symptoms of emotional disturbance or dysfunction. Just as the checking of physical symptoms comes as second nature to physicians, so also must they be constantly looking for symptoms of mental and emotional pain. When such symptoms are present, physicians can with integrity refer to programs specifically designed to deal with mental and emotional anguish.

These types of programs must be developed so that adequate coverage is ensured for the general population. Hospitals should provide these services as part of their community service programs.

Health-care professionals can cooperate by referral to hospital-based programs, or they can create their own programs within clinics and private practice. Groups of physicians can create these programs and refer patients to a central location. There should be departments of preventive medicine in treatment and rehabilitation centers, hospitals, and clinics.

The medical profession must incorporate preventive medicine as a full-fledged department within schools of medicine. Prevention techniques must be included within the curriculum for medical students. Medical schools and societies must sponsor continuing education for current professionals who desire to extend their expertise and practice into preventive medicine.

Many patients seeking medical attention have entered the physician's office with preexisting emotional difficulties. As it now stands, those patients will leave having received a thorough physical examination. Also, most of them will have received little or no attention to the signs and symptoms of their emotional distress. Patient and physician alike must begin to develop the mindset that focuses on emotional distress and problems such as obesity control, stress reduction, smoking control, nutrition, exercise, meditation, and biofeedback . All these must be incorporated into preventive medicine.

Chemical dependency treatment centers provide a strong base from which to develop the appropriate training programs that will enable social service agency personnel to increase their efforts in chemical dependency prevention. Agencies should avail themselves of the opportunity to cooperate in this training.

These four systems (education, social service, religion, and health care) are present throughout this country. All four may not be present in the smallest village, but for that village these systems are available at the county level. These four systems are present in our towns, cities, and metropolitan areas. In most cases, efforts in the prevention of chemical dependency are absent. In most instances, these systems have not implemented efforts in the prevention of chemical dependency, and, where they have, each system tends to operate unrelated to the others. Each system tends to operate as though it were isolated from the rest of the world.

Serious efforts to prevent chemical dependency must be undertaken on a cooperative basis. No one system can do everything. No one congregation, or agency, or school, or hospital has the resources to conduct by itself a comprehensive prevention program. Even if a single system did have the resources, it does not cover a broad enough base of the population. Effective prevention efforts must be comprehensive.

Each of the four systems must develop prevention efforts that are interdependent with the other systems as illustrated in Figure 16. Each system must assess its financial, physical, and human resources, and implement prevention efforts in concert with other participating systems. There is no reason for a local congregation, or a local school, or hospital, or social service agency to duplicate services. It is imperative that cooperation and collaboration become realized within the systems.

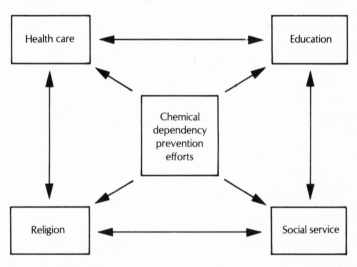

Figure 16

A local community has every right to expect that its schools, social agencies, congregations, and hospital would cooperate to provide a comprehensive teaching and counseling program as a resource for the local population. The competency of program leadership must be developed so that the population will have trust and confidence. Leadership in these four systems should develop and realize intersystem referrals based on competence of service offered. This type of collaboration would work to the mutual benefit of all people concerned, because the goal is to develop those counseling and teaching programs that result in the further development of individual value systems, positive self-images, competency in interpersonal relationships, development of sufficient coping mechanisms, and the ability to live with normal amounts of anxiety.

26 Next Step—Now!

Regardless of geogrphical location, prevention programs must be available to the general public. The populations of rural communities, small towns, cities, and metropolitan areas have every right to expect public-serving agencies to develop and provide services that result in the prevention of chemical dependency.

St. Mary's is working within these systems. It is exciting to see cooperation among educators, clergy, and social service and medical professionals as they develop and deliver programs that enhance individual health. New programs are being developed all over the country.

Unfortunately, there remain areas where prevention efforts are not present. In some cases, this absence of competent programming is the result of misinformed opinion; people in leadership positions refuse to organize programs because they mistakenly believe chemical dependency is not a major social problem. Some communities have no prevention programs because efforts and money are directed to law enforcement and education under the name of prevention. There continues to exist a general punitive attitude toward those suffering the disease of chemical dependency. Misinformation and punitive attitudes will not lower the rate of chemical dependency. In fact, there is evidence to suggest that the opposite occurs; misinformation and a punitive attitude increase the prevalence of chemical dependency.

We at St. Mary's believe the tide is turning. We believe attitudes are changing and prevention programs will be created at an increasing rate. We are doing everything possible to engourage this. Public and private agencies are now paying more attention to the problems associated with chemical dependency. Governmental units and private organizations are becoming more aware of their important roles. Research, study, and experience will further the development of even more effective prevention.

This work requires the support and involvement of concerned citizens. Each of us who leans the facts about chemical dependency and begins to act on that knowledge contributes to the betterment of our communities. We must share our knowledge and understanding. We must encourage and, if necessary, persuade the public-serving agencies to cooperate in the development and administration of health-producing programs.

There is much you can do. The tools and the knowledge are available. If your community does not have a prevention program, then talk with the leaders of public-serving agencies and find out why it doesn't exist. Encourage them to develop social policies that will lead to the organization and administration of prevention programs serving all segments of your community.

Give your support to those agencies and those people who are willing to work for the establishment of prevention programs serving your community and restoring health to people who are suffering.

Learn as much as you can and be involved in the development of prevention programs that focus on using existing resources. These resources are more than money. It takes the time of people to develop, organize, and continue prevention programs. It requires talent and skill. It takes space and access to people who need help. Locate the resources in your community that can be applied to the task. Identify the outside assistance you need and secure it. Federal and state agencies are prepared to help you. Private agencies, such as St. Mary's, are creatively working in communities and remain available to work wherever possible for the resolution of personal and social problems created by chemical dependency.

However, keep in mind that prevention efforts must not be seen as the only task. Effective treatment must also be available. Too many people are already suffering the disease of chemical dependency. For these people, for their families and friends, there is a clear message of hope — it is possible to successfully treat chemical dependency. Through treatment, people do regain productive and meaningful lives.

The steps of intervention have been outlined above (see Chapter

11). When they are followed, the opportunity exists for directing a person into diagnosis. Intervention has enabled thousands of people to begin the initial steps toward recovery. Intervention is a very serious process. It must be undertaken with care and forethought; but when it is accomplished, it results in movement toward health, new life, and happiness.

Diagnosis of chemical dependency has been tried and tested. It has been refined and sophisticated. It is now possible to confirm the presence or absence of chemical dependency within an individual. This breakthrough permits the patient and the diagnostician a degree of confidence unknown ten years ago. Unfortunately, in some sections of our country diagnosis is still unknown. Chemically dependent people are still denied access to effective treatment because they are being treated for physical and psychiatric disorders resulting from chemical dependency, but they are not being treated for the primary cause of their physical and emotional ill-health.

Treatment for the disease of chemical dependency must be available to all who need it. Where treatment is present, people recover. They do regain the ability to laugh and love and work. They do experience a quality of life and a sense of serenity that was previously impossible. These things are possible. They are happening every day at St. Mary's.

Appendix

Appendix

The contents of this Appendix are offered for information. The forms included are used by St. Mary's Adult Chemical Dependency Treatment Unit. They can be easily adapted for use by other programs.

The Twelve Steps of Alcoholics Anonymous

We:

ONE   admitted we were powerless over alcohol--that our lives had become unmanageable.

TWO   came to believe that a power greater than ourselves could restore us to sanity.

THREE   made a decision to turn our will and our lives over to the care of God as we understand Him.

FOUR   made a searching and fearless inventory of ourselves.

FIVE   admitted to God, to ourselves, and to another human being, the exact nature of our wrongs.

SIX   were entirely ready to have God remove all these defects of character.

SEVEN   humbly asked Him to remove our shortcomings.

EIGHT   made a list of all persons we had harmed, and became willing to make amends to them all.

NINE   made direct amends to such people wherever
            possible, except when to do so would
            injure them or others

TEN   continued to take personal inventory and
            when we were wrong promptly admitted it.

ELEVEN   sought through prayer and meditation to
            improve our conscious contact with God as we
            understood Him, praying only for knowledge
            of His will for us and the power to carry
            that out.

TWELVE   Having a spiritual awakening as the result
            of these steps, we try to carry this message
            to alcoholics, and to practice these
            principles in all our affairs.

St. Mary's Rehabilitation Center
Adult Chemical Dependency Treatment Unit

SAMPLE FAMILY INFORMATION SHEET

It is our privilege to be working with a member of your family,
but we need your assistance in getting to know the patient from
your view point as well as from his.

We feel very strongly that alcoholism is a family illness.
When family members become involved in the recovery process
right away, treatment can be more effective.

Please provide the requested information and return the sheet
to us as soon as possible. It is very important to have at
this juncture of treatment.

PATIENT'S NAME _____ DATE _____
              (last name)   (first)

YOUR NAME _____RELATIONSHIP TO PATIENT_____

1. KINDS OF CHEMICALS USED--Alcohol: beer, wine, hard
    liquor. PRESCRIPTION DRUGS: marijuana, speed, heroin, LSD,
    etc. OVER THE COUNTER DRUGS: antacids, bromides, cough
    syrup, pain relievers.

    _____
    _____

    AMOUNTS USED
    _____
    _____

    FREQUENCY OF USE
    _____
    _____

2. CHEMICAL USAGE PATTERN--alone, with others, morning use,
    afternoon use, evening use, daily, weekend, periodic.

    _____
    _____
    _____
    _____

3. ABUSE OF FAMILY--verbal and/or physical. Be specific.

    _____
    _____
    _____
    _____

4. INTERFERENCE IN FAMILY LIFE DUE TO THE USE OF ALCOHOL,
    pills, or other chemicals--worries, broken promises,
    arguments, irresponsibility, changing relationships, etc.

    _____
    _____
    _____
    _____

5. PHYSICAL PROBLEMS caused by the use of alcohol, pills or
    other chemicals

    _____
    _____

6. EFFECTS OF CHEMICAL USE ON WORK PERFORMANCE--decreased
    productivity/efficiency, increased "sick" days, reprimands,
    etc.

    _____
    _____

7. EFFECTS OF CHEMICAL USE UPON YOUR FINANCIAL SITUATION

    _____

8. Can you foresee anything that might interfere with the
    evaluation/treatment here of your family member?

    _____
    _____

9. Do you have reason(s) to believe your family member is
    chemically dependent?
    Yes_____   No_____   Not sure _____
    Explain: _____
    _____

10. Other comments you would like to make at this time

    _____
    _____
    _____
    _____
    _____
    _____

                    St. Mary's Rehabilitation Center
              Adult Chemical Dependency Treatment Unit

                     SAMPLE ADMISSION NOTES

B____ T____ P____ R____	Name_____
Height____ Weight____	Date of Birth____ Age____
How Pt. Admitted: Ambulatory__	Sex____ Physician____
Wheelchair____ Cart_____	Lifestyle____ Religion__
	Children_____

Accompanied by _____   Transferred From _____
Why are you here?_____
Referred by (courts, doctor, counselor, agency)_____

Observations

Apparent mental state _____
Behavior during admission _____
Is pt. under influence of a chemical? _____What?_____
Personal appearance _____
Remarks_____

Belongings checked by _____Valuables _____
Articles removed _____
Orientation to ATU_____Reading material given_____
Detox_____ To_____
Medical History: Do you have or have you had any of the
following:

	Yes	No		Yes	No
1. Heart attack_____			19. Ulcers _____		
2. Chest pain_____			20. Liver probs._____		
3. High B.P._____			21. Gallbladder probs._		
4. Stroke_____			22. Cancer_____		
5. Diabetes_____			23. Ear, nose, throat_		
6. Anemia_____			24. Eye probs._____		
7. Prolonged bleeding_			25. Psych. probs._____		
8. Emphysema_____			26. Nervous probs._		
9. Allergies_____			27. Suicide attempts_		
10. Asthma_____			28. Convulsions_____		
11. Shortness of breath_			29. Hallucinations_____		
12. Blood clots_____			30. Blackouts_____		
13. Arthritis_____			31. D.T.'s_____		
14. Bone or joint probs.			32. Shakiness_____		
15. Kidney or bladder prob._			33. Pregnancy (current)		
16. V.D._____			34. Gout_____		
17. Irreg. or prolonged periods_____			35. Skin problems_____		
18. Thyroid_____			36. Other		

If yes, write problem number and explain:_____

_____

_____

_____

_____

List past hospitalizations (most recent first)

Where	When	Why	Doctor

Are you taking medication at this time?

What	Dosage	For how long

Chemical History

Do you feel you have a problem with alcohol? _____Other drugs?_

How long_____Itemize other drugs used below:

_____

_____

	What	Dosage	How long used	When
Prescriptions:				
Street drugs:				
Over the counter:				

Have you ever mixed these drugs: _____What combinations?____
                                          Drug of choice_____
Have you had previous treatment for alcoholism/chemical
dependency? Yes ____No____

Where	When	How long abstinent

Have you ever attended A.A. or any other groups? Where, when and for how long?

When did you last use any alcohol?_____How much?_____

Other drugs?_____How much?_____

Do you have a history of:

	Yes	No			Yes	No
1. Preoccupation			6. Morning use			
2. Solitary use			7. Protecting supply			
3. Using as a medicine			8. Blackouts			
4. Hiding supply			9. Unplanned use			
5. Tolerance change			10. Rapid intake			

At this time, what is your usual daily intake or pattern of alcohol?_____Other drugs?_____

Signature:_____

Date:_____

St. Mary's Rehabilitation Center
Adult Chemical Dependency Treatment Unit

SAMPLE PATIENT INFORMATION

Name_____Age___Sex____Date of birth_____
Address_____City_____State_____
Phone_____Nature of address (home, apt., etc.)_____
Marital status_____Children_____Religion_____
Date admitted _____Counselor_____Physician_____
Referred by (courts, doctor, counselor, agency) _____
Occupation _____Employed by_____How long_____
Military _____Discharge_____Disability_____
Education_____Yrs._____Trade school_____Other training_____
County social worker _____Phone _____
Probation officer_____Phone_____
Industrial counselor _____Phone_____

Chemical History

Do you have a drug problem/alcohol _____Other drugs_____Both____
List name of drugs _____
How long alcohol_____How long drugs_____How long
has alcohol--drugs been a problem_____How has it been
a problem _____
Drug of choice_____Street drugs_____Over-counter___
Prescription drugs _____
Usage pattern:_____
Preoccupation __Solitary use__Use as a medicine__Hide supply__
Tolerance change ___ Morning use __ Tremors __Protect supply__
Gulp drinks__Unplanned use __Rapid intake __Blackouts ___
D.T.'s __Hallucinations__Seizures _____
Medical/psychological problems _____

Previous hospitalization for chemical abuse _____

Previous hospitalizations (psych, gastritis, liver, etc.)_____

How long chemically free after hospitalizations _____
Psychological problems _____
Nervous problems _____
Suicide attempts or thoughts _____
Medications _____
Sexual worries_____
Financial problems_____
Do you foresee anything that will interfere with your treatment
here_____

Family History

Number of children in your family ___Which child were you _____
Did anyone in your family have a problem with chemicals_____

Who_____
Did they recover_____
Method used_____
Who will be your concerned person during treatment _____
Address_____Phone _____

Self-Help

A.A._____When_____How long sober_____
Do yo have a sponsor?_____
Comments_____
Date _____ Counselor's signature _____

St. Mary's Rehabilitation Center
Adult Chemical Dependency Treatment Unit

SAMPLE TREATMENT PLAN

TREATMENT	DATE OR FRQNCY. PROJECTED	COMMENTS
Group therapy		
Individual therapy		
Recreational therapy		
Peer socialization		
Physical therapy____		
Bibliotherapy____		
A.A.____		
Relaxation therapy____		
Lectures____		
1st Step presentation____		
2nd/3rd Step conference		
4th Step preparation____		
5th Step conference____		
Conjoint family therapy		
Pastoral care____		
Grief care____		
T.A.____		
Biofeedback____		
Family conference____		
Employer conference____		
Probation officer conference____		
Social worker conference____		
Other____		

Patient signature _____
Pastoral care signature _____
Nursing signature _____
Counselor signature_____

St. Mary's Rehabilitation Center
Adult Chemical Dependency Treatment Unit

Sample Discharge Plan

1. Discharge to home or apartment or halfway house	
2. AA--Aftercare Growth Group--Aftercare	
3. AA--Community level	
4. Narcotics Anonymous	
5. Additional step work	
6. Sponsor	
7. Further primary treatment	
8. Outpatient program	
9. Seek employment	
10. Return to present job	
11. Vocational counseling	
12. Couples communication	
13. Marriage counseling	
14. Further counseling (type)	
15. Return visit (out-of-town pt.)	
16. Other	

Date_____Counselor's signature_____

St. Mary's Rehabalitation Center
Adult Chemical Dependency Treatment Unit

<u>Sample Daily Schedule</u>

This will be your schedule for the first few days you are
here. Please keep it with you and add to it as your schedule
is expanded.

7:00	Arise
7:15	Temperature--In Wing Lounges
7:30	Breakfast for 4th Floor; 7:40 Breakfast for 3rd Floor-- 1st Floor lDining Room
8:00	Medications--Nurses' Desk--Nurse will tell you what other times
8:15	Physical therapy when assigned by Doctor
8:45	Group or lecture on Family Day only
9:00	Lecture--3rd Floor Lecture Room
9:30	
10:00	Group
10:30	4th Step prep--when assigned by counselor
11:30	Lunch for 4th Floor; 11:40 Lunch for 3rd Floor--1st Floor Dining Room
12:00	Blood pressure--Nurses' Desk
1:00	Lecture--3rd Floor Lecture Room
1:45	T.A. on Wednesday if assigned by doctor
2:00	1st Step group or jone-to-one with counselor
3:00	
3:30	Blood pressure--Nurses' Desk
3:45	Physical therapy when assigned by doctor
4:00	Outside recreational activities
4:15	Physical therapy when assigned by doctor
5:00	
5:45	Dinner for 4th Floor; 5:55 Dinner for 3rd Floor--1st Floor Dining Room
6:30	Visiting hours
7:00	Lecture--3rd Floor Lecture Room
8:00	Blood pressure--Nurses' Desk
9:00	
9:30	Relaxation group--2nd Floor Chapel
10:00	
12:00	All patients in respective rooms

Your weekend schedule is somewhat different--Please check the
Unit Bulletin Board.